No Regrets
The Autobiography of
László Veres

No Regrets
The Autobiography of
László Veres

with a Foreword by George R. Hanson
Musical Director, Tucson Symphony Orchestra

The Patrice Press
Tucson, Arizona

Copyright © 2003
by László Veres

All rights reserved.

Library of Congress Cataloging in Publication Data

Veres, László, 1937-
    No regrets: the autobiography of László Veres.
        p. cm.
    ISBN 1-880397-49-8
    1. Veres, László, 1937- 2. Band directors--Arizona--Biography. I. Title.

ML422.V48 A3
784'.092--dc21
[B]
                                        2003045748

The Patrice Press
PO Box 85639
Tucson, AZ 85754-5639
1-800-367-9242
Email: books@patricepress.com
www.patricepress.com

Printed in the United States of America

To Michael, André, and Daniel

Contents

Foreword	vii
Preface and Acknowledgments	ix
1 Under Nazi and Soviet Rule	1
2 Soccer Years	20
3 The Lure of Music	27
4 Hungary Revolts	33
5 Hungary Repressed	42
6 Fleeing the Iron Curtain	46
7 To the Land of the Free	52
8 Life in America	67
9 The U.S. Army	83
10 Linda Sue Ward	97
11 To Tucson	114
12 The Tucson Symphony Orchestra	125
13 Santa Rita High School	137
14 Picking up the Baton	145
15 Mary McGrath	161
16 Arizona Symphonic Winds	171
17 John Philip Veres, King of the Tucson Bandstand	188
18 Frances Ann Upham	196
19 Béla and Klára Veres	207
Epilogue	212

Foreword

Tucsonans became acquainted with László Veres decades ago, long before I came to this wonderful city of Tucson. It is always a joyful experience to see him walk briskly to his podium, raise his baton, and turn to his audience to join him in singing our National Anthem. That broad smile seems to telegraph a lot of love for his thousands of fans, and he must feel that love coming right back to him. We see that, too, when he guest-conducts our Tucson Symphony Orchestra and the many other musical groups in our town.

People may think that they know László very well. As it turns out, most of them really don't know him at all. Not until he produced this amazing autobiography could anyone realize what an incredible life he has led.

"Incredible" is a strong word. But consider this: as a youngster he suffered the horror of seeing his neighbors routed from their Budapest homes by the Nazis, never to be seen again. He grew up fearing for his life and the lives of his family, as the ruthless Soviets replaced the German regime. You can follow him as he escaped from behind the Iron Curtain, on foot, into Austria in the middle of the night. You can feel his anguish as he searched for the brother who had fled earlier, somewhere in the West.

László had been a champion soccer player in Hungary—very

near world class. He attended a trade school to become a talented automobile mechanic. He struggled mightily to become an American after coming to our country, unable to speak the language. His determination to master the clarinet was so intense that he was admitted to America's finest conservatories of music, and later won the clarinet chair in our Tucson Symphony Orchestra.

László has conducted more than a hundred concerts of his Arizona Symphonic Winds at Tucson's Udall Park. At the conclusion of each of them he points his baton to his timpanist. A thunderous roll starts "America the Beautiful." He turns to his audience, sees them standing in joyful reverence, and they all sing with him. When those audiences read his life story, I think that they will learn what it really means to be an American.

George R. Hanson, Musical Director
Tucson Symphony Orchestra

Preface and Acknowledgments

While a soldier in the United States Army stationed at Fort Huachuca, Arizona, I was befriended by one of the high-ranking officers on base, Col. Robert Fisher and his wife, in 1961. I was a member of the 36th Army Band and also played in the dance band even though I preferred performing the classics instead of the popular type music. The dance band performed on many functions in the officers' club that included background music for dinners and dances. One night during break Colonel Fisher overheard me talking with a fellow bandsman and was interested in finding out where my accent came from. I told him that I was born in Hungary. After the final number as we were packing up our instruments he approached me again and introduced me to his wife. They asked me if I would be available to come to their home one evening for dinner. I accepted their gracious invitation. During dinner we had some small talk, however, eventually the conversation shifted towards my life's history as they were asking me more and more questions.

Just as I was ready to leave he asked me if I would be willing to give a short talk reflecting about my life in Hungary to the congregation of the church he and his wife belonged to. He asked me if I would be agreeable to share my experiences about growing up in a country that witnessed World War II and about the living conditions behind the Soviet-controlled Iron Curtain. He was well aware of the fact that my knowledge and use of the English language was limited and I had difficulty with it. Nonetheless, that didn't trouble him or his wife.

One day the three of us drove to Tucson and I presented some of my life history to the attentive audience. Many years later as I look back, I question how much of what I said was understood, since my accent was very thick at the time (still is) and my English left much to be desired. I spoke about the war and the bombings as I remembered them; spoke about the heroism of my parents and the hardships they had to endure; talked about my brothers, and mentioned my escape from Hungary after the 1956 revolution. I was shocked at the unbelievable ovation and prolonged applause I received at the end of my talk. That was the beginning of the many talks I have given in the past forty-plus years.

I became a band director in 1967 and in the classroom I have talked many times about my life experiences to my students throughout my teaching years. The more I talked the more they wanted to hear. Many parents came to see me, to meet the teacher who had slowly changed the life of their children for the better, for they were becoming more responsible, caring, respectful people. They wanted to know how I managed to make their children behave so well at home, something they were not used to. My answer was simple: "Most people in this country take too many things for granted and what this great nation has to offer is not being valued. Freedom of speech, freedom of the press, being freely able to move around, and having the privilege to vote was not available to the people where I came from. I had never seen nor tasted an orange nor a banana until I escaped to the west. Food was scarce and owning a car was only a dream."

These parents looked at me in puzzlement for they had never heard any of these things before. I continued, "I want my students to love their country and fight for the freedom they enjoy so their children and grandchildren can have a safe, fruitful life also. I want them to love their music, for the love of the fine arts will make them better human beings; I want them to respect their teachers, parents, friends; I want them to become good citizens and contributing members of the society. I emphasize and remind them frequently, that in this country one has the opportunity to become anything they want to be, and finally, the statement 'I can't' should be forever taken from their vocabulary."

People were constantly encouraging me to write down my life experiences to share it with others. I have been putting it off, didn't think anybody would actually be interested in it. Mary, mother of my sons André and Daniel, was also suggesting that. At one point I made a tape recording of my life in a short version, which was to be transferred to paper. I have no idea what happened to that tape.

In the early months of 2002, my nephew, Josh Béla Veres, son of my younger brother George, was writing about the Holocaust as a class assignment and needed information about the Veres family's survival during World War II. He asked his dad for information but since he was too young to remember those years he directed his son's questions to his uncle Zoltán (Zoli), being the oldest of the Veres brothers and having the most knowledge about that part of the past. My brother Zoli called me and asked me if I would write down a few facts and send the information to Josh Béla. I told him I would.

As I was writing, the paper got longer and longer and with the help of Zoli, our mother's, and my own recollection, I was reliving the past and conditions we lived in. After my wife Frances finished proofreading the twelve-page document it was mailed to Zoli, who in turn sent it to our nephew. Zoli was extremely impressed with the paper and wanted to know where I learned how to write in such format and so well. I didn't think it was that good. Both my wife Frances and my brother Zoli made copies of the paper and passed it on to their respective relatives to read.

I thought everything would stop right there but it didn't go that way. My wife suggested that I should continue writing, however, this time it should be about the life and the many experiences of László Veres, for the reason that my children Michael, André, and Daniel would have some knowledge about their heritage and would know something about their father that they may share it with their own children in future years. In the meantime my brother Stephen published an autobiographical book in the summer of 2002. This gave me the inspiration to finally put in writing what had been in my head for the past forty-some years. Frances made me sit down at the computer and slowly the writing began.

I am grateful for her encouragement and the many people who persuaded me to write and undertake this assignment. I want to thank Gregory and Kathy Franzwa, for the many hours they spent on proofreading the manuscript, and suggesting the idea of putting the text into a book format, my brother Zoli for all his invaluable information, and Frances for having confidence in me to complete this project. Most of all I would like to thank my parents; without them this would not have been possible.

This little book is dedicated to my children: Michael, André, and Daniel, in the hope that they might find some inspiration in me as I have in my own parents. I want them to know that I have always loved them and shall continue loving them forever.

April 2003
Tucson, Arizona

Timeline

1937	Born in Budapest on June 19
1943	Entered 1st grade in public school
1945	End of World War II
1949	Joined "MTK" soccer team at the entry level (12 years old)
1951	Finished 8th grade schooling in June
	Entered auto mechanic trade school in September (14 years old)
1953	Receive auto mechanic degree in May (not yet 16 years old)
	Started full time job as an auto mechanic
	Started clarinet lessons in the fall at the age of 16
1955	Selected into the Hungarian all-star soccer team, just below the "pro" level
1956	Auditioned and accepted into the Béla Bartók Conservatory of Music
	October 23, start of the Hungarian Revolution
	November 6, escaped from Hungary to Austria
	Lived and worked as a mechanic in Vienna until March 1957
1957	Arrived at McGuire Air Force Base in the USA on March 11
	Worked in Washington, D.C., as a mechanic for one week
	Moved to Cleveland and worked in a lamp factory until June
	Moved to Boston when parents arrived in the USA with my three younger brothers
	Worked as a mechanic for two different companies until I got fired from each for not speaking English
	Went to New York City to work as a carpenter and to play soccer for a professional Italian team
	Moved back to Boston in the fall, after being fired as a carpenter for not being a member of the Carpenters' Union
1958	Worked in a shoe factory for about 1° years
	Started night school to learn the English language
	Accepted as a student at the New England Conservatory of Music
1960	Drafted into the U.S. Army in August
	Stationed at Fort Huachuca, Arizona after basic training at Fort Benning, Georgia and Fort Gordon, Georgia

	At Ft. Huachuca played in the 36th Army Band
1962	Married to Linda Sue Ward
	Became a U.S. citizen on August 14 in Bisbee, Arizona
	Stationed in Fulda, Germany, about sixty kilometers from Frankfurt
	At Fulda, played in the Army Cavalry Band
1963	Michael Veres, son, born in Frankfurt, Germany
	Honorable discharge from the United States Army in August
	Entered University of Arizona as freshman in the fall
1966	Went to University of Oregon as a teaching assistant and worked on Masters program
	Received Bachelor of Music Education degree with distinction from University of Arizona in December
1967	First teaching position in Tombstone, Arizona, as director of bands
	Appointed principal clarinetist in Tucson Symphony Orchestra (16 yrs.)
1969	Moved to Tucson and became band director of the new Santa Rita High School (14 yrs.)
1972	Received Master of Music degree from University of Oregon
1975	Appointed conductor of the Tucson Symphony Youth Orchestra (1 year)
1976	Founder Music Director/Conductor of the newly formed Philharmonia Orchestra of Tucson (7 yrs.)
1977	Death of Béla Veres, our father, on July 3
1980	Appointed conductor of Arizona Touring Orchestra
1980	Appointed conductor of Simon Peter Orchestra in Tucson (18 yrs.)
1983	Leave of absence from TUSD, resigned from Tucson Symphony and Philharmonia Orchestras
1984	Divorce from first wife Linda, mother of Michael
1985	Band director at Palo Verde High School (1 yr.)
1986	Founder, Music Director/Conductor of Arizona Symphonic Winds concert band
1986	Band director at Rincon/University High School (1 yr.)
1987	Married to Mary McGrath
1987	André Veres, son, born in Tucson, Arizona

1987	Band director at Tucson High Magnet School (12 yrs.)
1988	Triple bypass open-heart surgery
1989	Daniel Veres, son, born in Tucson
1990	Established outdoor concerts at Udall Park with the Arizona Symphonic Winds
1990	Established and directed the famed Tucson High Steel Band (10 yrs.)
1993	Appointed Music Director/Conductor of Foothills Phil Orchestra
1993	Appointed Assistant Conductor Tucson Pops Orchestra
1998	Appointed Music Director/Conductor of Tucson Pops Orchestra
1999	Divorced from second wife, Mary McGrath, mother of André and Daniel
1999	Retired from public school teaching after thirty years
1999	Married to Frances Ann Upham July 24

No Regrets
The Autobiography of
László Veres

1

Under Nazi and Soviet Rule

Historical background

Béla Veres (our father, also known as Apú) was born on July 29, 1905 in Miskolc, a city located in the northeastern part of Hungary. He studied business as a trade. According to him, the Magyars can trace the Veres (pronounced VER-ish) name back to the founding of Hungary around 800 A.D. The original Veres was a high-ranking member of the military and was a wealthy landowner with status. My father died in Los Angeles, California, on July 3, 1977, at the age of seventy-one.

Klára Lerner (our mother, also known as Anyú) was born on March 17, 1912, in Budapest, Hungary. She was a seamstress. Her parents came from Poland. At the age of ninety-one she resides in Los Angeles, California.

Béla and Klára were married in 1931 or 1932 in Budapest. The wedding took place in a Jewish synagogue. The Veres side of the family never showed up for the wedding for they didn't approve of the marriage, as they were Protestants.

Father's father's, Veres István (my grandfather), was a bootmaker by trade. He died of malaria on the Italian front as a soldier during World War I. Father was about eleven years old when his father died. He loved his father very much during that short time. He told me more than once that he would use his ten fingernails willingly to dig him up from his grave if he could be alive again.

Father's mother's maiden name was Kóta Klára. Our "Nagyanyi," as we children called her, died in 1953 of cancer, at the age of about seventy. István and Klára had five children, but only four of them survived. The first one died at childbirth. The oldest was a boy named Béla (our father) followed by three girls: Irén, Bözsi, and Eta. Eta is the only one who had a child, a boy named Miklós, or Micú for short. Bözsi had a child, but it died at a very early age. Irén was childless, and I don't believe she ever married.

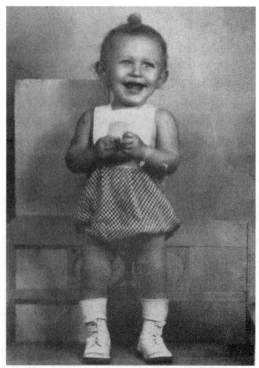

László Veres, age 1, Budapest

Under Nazi and Soviet Rule

All of our aunts are dead from this side of the family. Eta was my mother's favorite sister-in-law. Mother's parents were Rottler Miksa and Lerner Janka. Miksa was a tailor by trade. They were from Poland and settled in Budapest around the 1890s. Zoltán (or Zoli), László (or Laci), Stephen (István/Pista), George (György/Gyuri), and John (János/Jancsi) are the children of Béla and Klára Veres. Zoltán, my older brother, and I never bothered to anglicize our names, and I'm the only brother who insists that our family name be pronounced the Hungarian way. I was born on June 19, 1937, and I am the second oldest of the five boys.

We lived on the third floor of an apartment building at 15 Dobozi utca (street), VIII district of Budapest, Hungary, until early February 1945. I recall incidents from about 1943 on. Zoli was born on January 26, 1935; Pista on July 9, 1941; Gyuri October 26, 1943; and Jancsi on March 26, 1945, just a few months before the end of World War II. Jancsi never lived in that house. All of us boys were born in Budapest.

The Holocaust years and World War II

According to my elder brother Zoli, the Nazis took our maternal grandfather, Rottler Miksa, away and as they were marching the collected Jews toward the "Nazi Camps," he fell and broke his leg. Instead giving him medical help the Nazis shot him and left him dead. I didn't know this. The only thing I knew was that he disappeared one day. Zoli said that our grandfather is listed in Israel as murdered by the Nazis.

Our grandmother on mother's side, Rottler Lerner Janka, an orthodox Jew, survived the holocaust. According to mother, after Janka's husband was taken away she went into hiding in a small village. Both she and her husband were Jews from Poland and those Jews were rounded up early on, maybe in 1939-40. The

No Regrets

Nazis finally captured our grandma. She was dressed as an old woman (she wasn't) and told her captors that she was looking for her husband who had left her. The Nazis used her as a cook in their kitchen. The Nazis took her as German for she conversed with them in perfect German language (she spoke the "Hoch Deutsch" dialect, a type of dialect that is accepted by the Germans as the language of their country). She also spoke Polish, Yiddish, and Hungarian.

Our uncles, Ármin and Sámuel, mother's brothers, and her sister Baba also survived, including her husband Mihály/Misi. I'm not sure how, but I really believe that our father had something to do with their protection from the Nazis.

Our mother (Anyú) wore a yellow star on her overcoat every time she went out of the house to do errands. Zoli told me that he had a yellow star sewed on his overcoat also, according to mother. I did not know the significance of the yellow star as a six-year-old. However, it didn't take me long to learn that all Jews had to wear it during the Nazi occupation for easy identification purposes.

Our father (Apú) didn't have to wear one since he was Protestant (református) by birth, although he converted to Judaism when he married our mother (that was the condition to marry his bride). Father went through the circumcision ceremony at the age of twenty-six, which is an extremely dangerous procedure at that advanced age. According to mother, he almost died after the operation. (Today, the medical profession is more advanced technically, especially in the United States, compared to Hungary in the 1930s.) Uncle Misi, Baba's husband, helped him back to recovery. Obviously our future father loved his bride very much for he gave up his own religion and was willing to go through that painful operation.

This marriage caused father's side of the family to break away from him. They did not accept mother as a member of the family for a long time. The birth of their first child, Zoli, brought some peace between the newlyweds and father's side of the family.

It took a long time to accept our mother (if ever) as a member of the Veres family, with the exception of Eta, father's youngest sister. The Veres family thought that father married a lazy Jewish girl. How wrong they were!

Later in my life father told me, that he had never met nor seen a harder working Jewish or non-Jewish woman than our mother. He also said to me, "There is no one like her," and in front of me always talked about our mother as he would talk about "Istenröl" (God), with the greatest reverence, admiration and love.

My mother and father in 1951

Since our father didn't have a Jewish sounding last name, didn't look Jewish, and his birth certificate listed him as Protestant (also on the identification papers that one had to carry at all times), he was left alone, and this gave him opportunities to hide and protect Jews from the Nazis.

Now comes the important part of the survival of the Veres

family:
    In his younger years father wanted to become a Protestant minister and he entered the ministry school. (He told me this story much later in my life, when I was about thirty.) He quit the ministry school and went on to become an apprentice in the business field. When a Jewish mother gives birth to a child, the child automatically becomes a Jew regardless of the father's religion. All Veres boys were born as Jews. In those days the religion of the child was recorded on the birth certificate. Except for Jancsi, all the Veres boys' birth certificates indicated that we were Jews. (I'm not sure about Gyuri since he was born in October 1943, and Jancsi wasn't born yet.)
    One of father's friends from the ministry school was appointed minister in a church in Budapest not too far from our apartment. He went to see him seeking his help in changing the boy's birth certificates from Jewish to Protestant. I don't know who used what influence; the only thing I know is that at least my birth certificate paper was changed legally. (I don't know about the other brothers'.)
    On the same certificate father is listed as református (Protestant) and mother as Jew. I have my birth certificate from the Hungarian Government Agency in my possession dated June 19, 1943, while still showing my birth as June 19, 1937. Father had the great foresight to take actions early to protect his family from future tragedy. In 1943, father was thirty-eight and mother thirty-one years old.

My childhood years

    Mother told Zoli that the house we lived in had a yellow star painted on the front door. I did not know that. But I remember that in our apartment complex, the apartment on the first floor facing the street was empty, since the Nazis deported the Jewish family that used to live there. To deter the Nazis from coming into

Under Nazi and Soviet Rule

our apartment, father put up a Christmas tree right at the front window of the apartment, making the Nazis believe that the house had only Christians living in it. This was a risky move, since the whole neighborhood had a large Jewish population. I guess the plan worked, or at least helped.

    I have total recall of the following incident that took place in our apartment's courtyard:

    We were in the shelter (bunker) when three Nazis appeared in the courtyard (actually, they were the Hungarian "Nyilasok," members of the Nazi Party in soldier's uniforms) looking for Jews to be deported. Father went to greet them, flanked by Zoli on his left and me on his right, holding our hands tightly. Zoli was eight and I was six years old. We were facing the three of them, with their captain in the middle with a pistol in his hand and the other two on either side of him, with loaded machine guns on their shoulders. He asked them if he could be assistance to them, for which they replied that they were looking for hiding Jews. Father replied in a loud voice telling them that he was a true Hungarian and that he would not hide Jews. He said to Zoli: "Zoltán, szavald el nekük a 'Nemzeti dalt: Talpra Magyar' (recite for them the poem 'National Song: Rise up, Magyar') and let us show them that we are dedicated true Hungarians." Zoli jumped front of the Nazis and recited the poem (the poem has a very patriotic theme, was written and recited by Petofi Sándor, the great Hungarian poet and patriot, on the steps of the National Museum in Budapest on the eve of March 15, 1848, a day before the start of the Hungarian revolution staged against the Hapsburg Empire. I'll include the poem at the end of this document.) When Zoli was finished, he saluted the Nazis and grabbed father's hand. The soldiers left, and we went back to the bunker.

    In the summer of 1968 (I was thirty-one years old) I was talking to father and reminded him of this incident. He told me that he had total recollection of this, and said that after we got back to the bunker he had to change his pants for he soiled them from being so scared. He took a tremendous chance on his, his family's, and the rest of the Jews' lives that he was protecting. As I recall, he did not look scared to me at all, but the bravest of the brave! After watching the movie "The Music Box" a few years ago, it suddenly occurred to me that we were as close to death as one could be, for Nazis did not hesitate to shoot people on the spot. (Every one of the Veres' should see this movie, with the exception of our mother, for she lived through it in real life and has seen enough).

As mother told me years ago, when I was born and she found out that I was a boy she started to cry. I was the second child and she wanted a little girl. My parents tried again and another boy, Pista, was born. Than came another boy, Gyuri, and finally the last boy, Jancsi. Mother also told me that one day she was all dressed up and was ready to leave the apartment with her sister Baba, when father walked in unexpectedly and asked her where they were going. Mother said they are going to see a doctor because she didn't want another child due to the struggling conditions our family was in. Father's reply was that if we can feed and take care of three children, we'd be able to take care of one more. By not aborting the pregnancy, the newborn baby, Gyuri, born in October 1943, would live to become a very important part in the future of the Veres family.

Mother told me that all her friends and relatives were talking about "poor Klára" having five children and that she must be crazy. "Let them feel sorry for me. I don't feel sorry for myself for I love all of my children." Later on in her life the same people were telling her, "Klára, you have such beautiful five boys who love you. How lucky you are!" She also told me, that without any hesitation, she would re-live her life again, bringing five boys into this world under the same difficult living conditions. She has absolutely no regrets for she takes the greatest pride in her children and her husband.

Mother's recollection of the following incident was told recently to Zoli:

Under Nazi and Soviet Rule

Mother was taken away by the Gestapo (Nazis) and was put in a camp called "Tatárza." Father took us children, Zoli, Pista, Gyuri and me to the gates of the camp. He was holding Gyuri in his arms while the rest of us were standing next to him. This was around May 1944. Zoli was nine, I was a month shy of seven, Pista two months shy of three and Gyuri was seven months old. How strangely does destiny work? An announcement came through the loudspeaker telling all mothers to step aside if they can prove that they have a child less than one year of age. As luck would have it mother saw us children with father holding Gyuri in his arms, went to tell the captain that her husband at the gate was holding her seven-month-old child. When they let our mother out of the camp father told her: "Nobody, not even God, will ever take you away from me again." Mother was thirty-two years old at that time. She has prayed and thanked God many times for not aborting her pregnancy, her husband for his decision, encouragement, and wisdom, for her pregnancy with Gyuri had saved her life, and in turn gave us children a loving mother who took care of us with her caring and loving husband.

Air raids

During the air raids the sirens would go off, signaling that everybody should get into the bomb shelter (bunker) located under the apartment as quickly as possible, because the incoming allied airplanes were bombing. It seems to me that those air raids always took place in the middle of the night, although a bomb destroyed our apartment in the daytime. We had to dress very quickly (it was winter and as I remember it was always cold) and in the total darkness we had to find our way to safety climbing down the steps from the third floor to the bunker. On these occasions, as a six- or seven-year-old, my assignment was to grab one handle of the laundry basket, Zoli the other handle, and carry the basket down with Gyuri in it. Father carried Pista and mother was carrying Jancsi in her stomach. Many days the sirens went off often, and at times like those we just stayed in the bunker. Father built a nice little cubicle for us at one corner of the bunker. We spent many nights there squeezed in with our neighbors like a bunch of sardines, but we children didn't care since we didn't know any other way. We also spent lots of nights with rats, spiders, and many other more friendly creatures.

During the air raids, airplanes were dropping bombs on all the bridges that were connecting Pest with Buda, and on railroads, water supply tanks, and buildings everywhere. One day there was a tremendous explosion above us, for one of those bombs hit our building, completely wiping out the side where our apartment was, losing most of our belongings. The dust and panic was everywhere. Women were putting wet towels and handkerchiefs around our faces to protect us children from breathing in all that dust. All the adults acted incredibly fast to protect one another, especially the children. Amazingly, no one got killed, to the best of my knowledge.

After the bombing we were forced to stay in the bunker. There was no water available so father decided that a hole should be dug to find water. As the opening got deeper some of us children were put to work for we were small enough to fit into the hole to scrape up the soil from the bottom and pass it up in a bucket. As we were reaching wet ground someone ran in yelling that heavy snowflakes were falling outside. The digging stopped, for all of a sudden there was drinking water available from the snow! Our thirst was quenched and the adults started to collect snow into buckets for future use.

End of World War II

The Soviet Red Army was coming into Budapest during the early part of January 1945, pushing the Germans back to Germany. The Russian foot soldiers were going from house to house sweeping the enemy out of their hiding places. One early morning

Under Nazi and Soviet rule

the shelter door was kicked in and a couple of Russian soldiers were standing in the doorway with machine guns pointing and screaming, "Germansky!, Germansky!" looking for German soldiers. One of the alarm clocks went off to their right and caused them to get frightened. They emptied a great amount of bullets in the direction of the alarm clock smashing everything in its way. Luckily, no human was killed. Father told them "no Germansky here" and offered them something to drink including some perfume, which they drank. Zoli told me that the soldiers made him hold up a candle because they were looking for women to rape. In the dark the women were covering themselves with dark material to make them look old and not to look desirable to the sexually excited soldiers. As I remember, those Russian soldiers were from the region close to Mongolia, judging by their faces. Eventually they left.

To pass time more pleasantly, father with the other surviving neighbors built a theater stage in the courtyard and people got on stage to act, and to provide some form of entertainment for all of us. As I recall, some of them were really funny. In one of the acts, a man and a woman were looking in each other's hair looking for *tetü* (lice), which was plentiful those days. (I remember our parents constantly checking our heads for those parasites and having our heads washed with petrol many times, carrying the unpleasant smell with us for what seemed to be a long time.) A large piece of rug was hanging from the floor above the stage acting as a curtain. When the show was ready to start the rug was pulled up to let the show begin.

Soon after the Russian soldiers left, father was building a box about three feet wide, four and a half feet long and three feet deep. He then proceeded to attach it to a sled we had. Mother was put inside the box with Pista and Gyuri and some of our possessions, which weren't many. With a bunch of blankets, they were covered to keep them warm. Mother was pregnant and was getting very close to delivering the new baby. (Jancsi was born in March.) This was around the middle of February of 1945, about two months before the end of the war in Hungary. World War II did not officially end until the summer of 1945. Father bought a house years before in Rákoscsaba, an outlying district of Budapest, for his mother. His mother and two of his sisters lived there with their families. The winter was very cold. The snow under our feet was powdery and cracking. Cold or not, we hit the road with father pulling the loaded sled with a cord over his shoulder with Zoli and I pushing with all of our might. I was pushing in the back, while Zoli being older and stronger was on the side at the edge of the road holding the loaded sled from turning over. Rákoscsaba is about sixteen kilometers (ten miles) from our apartment. In the middle of nowhere a truck approached us from the opposite direction, loaded with Russian soldiers. One of the soldiers threw a loaf of bread to us. The fresh bread landed in the snow, we picked it up and had something to eat, maybe for the first time that day. We made it to our grandmother's house and I'm positive that everyone was exhausted. We stayed there until May or June, 1945.

One day our parents disappeared, and a few days later father returned to us riding on a military truck and as he was leaping off with a happy voice he was yelling to all of us, "Egy fiú! egy fiú gyerek!" (It's a boy! it's a boy!)

Life after the war and the communist years

The war was over. One-day father told Zoli and me to get dressed. We carried with us a mid-size pitcher full of cooked beans and were headed out to the Rákoscsaba train station. The train arrived and it was full, with people hanging out everywhere. Somehow father got on the train, opened a window, and Zoli and I were passed up to him. All three of us were in the lavatory and that is where we stayed until we arrived at the "Keleti" (East) train station in Budapest. Father locked the door and the window and wouldn't let anybody in during the travel.

Under Nazi and Soviet Rule

We walked to our new apartment building (I'm not sure if the streetcars were running) carrying with us the beans, a loaf of bread, and salt. Our new residence was located at 21 Karácsony Sándor utca 4th floor (in Hungary the first floor equals second floor in the United States). This was a luxury apartment by Hungarian standards with three bedrooms, kitchen, long hallway, bathroom, and a small room off the kitchen area where the maid slept. For a short time we had a maid. When we entered our new living quarters, father cut a piece of bread for each of us and put lots of salt on it. Later in life, I told mother about this and she said that it is a Jewish tradition. I view it differently: the salty bread made us kids thirsty and by drinking lots of water our stomach was full, and for a while we had no hunger pains. The apartment was totally empty with the exception of one mattress on the floor and that is where we all slept. One day the rest of the family arrived and slowly we got some furniture. By September Zoli and I were attending school. Zoli was ten, I was eight, Pista four, Gyuri two, and Jancsi a few months old. Life was going on.

The doors to our apartment in Budapest

There was a bakery down the street from us. It was closed, for the owners had been taken away by the Nazis. (I think their

Our Budapest apartment was on the top floor of this building–the first two windows from the right. My bed was next to the second window. One day a bullet entered there, starting a fire in my pillow.

The Veres brothers in 1947. From left, back row– László (age 10) and Zoli. Front row–Gyuri, Jancsi, and Pista.

Under Nazi and Soviet Rule

The Veres brothers in 1951. Left to right–László, Gyuri, Jancsi, Pista, and Zoli.

name was Engel). Father somehow reopened the bakery and with the help of others fired up the ovens, baking bread again, and provided the all-important food for the neighborhood. The bakery was producing bread day and night to keep up with the demand. Food was scarce. I remember being in the bakery with Zoli and possibly with Pista helping with the work. I'm not sure if we were much help, although I do remember taking bread out of the oven with a wooden spatula that had a long handle on it. The smell was great and the freshly baked bread tasted delicious. People brought with them a pot full of uncooked beans to be baked in the oven. For lack of available storage place the baked beans were stored on the floor until the costumers claimed them. One day one of the adult helpers stepped into one of the pots, kicking over everything. We kids were laughing. He wasn't, and neither was our father. As Jancsi would say, "Can't he take a joke?"

The bakery business stopped when a man named Hidas

turned father in to the police for being against the Jews during the Nazi occupation. He was put in jail, but at the trial a few days later he was acquitted and released. Jews from the neighborhood showed up at the trial testifying in father's behalf. They told the judge that because of Béla Veres, they are alive today, for he hid them and protected them from the Nazis.

Our parents tried lots of small business ventures including selling calendars, salt, cián köt (pesticide), and cooking oil at the market (at Teleki tér). Zoli tells me that his job was to pull a four-wheel cart to the market carrying the merchandise. After closing he had to pull it again and deposit it at grandmother's apartment, for they had a horse barn and that is where it was kept. Zoli also told me that while he was pulling, his friends were playing soccer and making fun of him. (I'm pretty sure that Zoli had a few chosen words for them). During the Christmas season decorative ornaments were sold by our parents in the warehouse building (Vásárcsarnok) located at the bank of the river Danube (Duna). A stand was set up by father right next to vendors who sold fish. There were many customers in that area. To attract more and more customers father always decorated our stand skillfully, making it beautifully attractive to the buyers. Zoli and I were helping, especially Zoli, for he was a great salesman, while I was very shy. (Pista was also a good salesman, working as a helper in a small grocery store next to our home, called Ádler. Pista was extremely well liked there.)

It was always very cold at the warehouse and we did lots of moving around (jumping, etc.) to keep ourselves warm. During the spring and summer months mother would get old bicycle tubes and cut rubber bands out of them, selling them to housewives at the market. They were to be used for many different jobs, mainly 'dúnsztólni' (putting up cooked tomatoes or different type of cooked fruits to make jams in glass containers, to be preserved for the winter months). They used rubber bands to tighten down the cellophane wrap that covered the top. I can still hear clearly mother's voice at the market: "Aszzonyok, Asszonyok, kötözö gumik, vegyennek kötözö gumit." (Ladies, ladies, rubber bands, buy rubber bands). She tried many different things in her lifetime with her husband to augment the family income, and it was always for the children. As I write and think about these incidences, I can't help but have tears in my eyes. I totally admire my parent's bravery, guts, and smarts to find ingenious ways to scrape a penny here, a penny there, for the family's survival. I do not know how to thank them for the incredible sacrifices they made for us children.

Soon after the war many of the theaters that didn't get damaged opened up and shows were presented to the public. I had a chance to see many operettas and other productions. My parents encouraged us to attend the performances. Years later I realized that the theaters were encouraged because for a few hours people forgot about their troubles, and even if it was for a short time, we were transferred to a dream world. I especially loved the operettas for their beautiful melodies and make-believe stories. One day my father got a ticket for me to attend the performance of the "János Vitéz" operetta in the Erkel Opera House. I was carried away with the beautiful music and the magic that was created on stage. At another time he got me a ticket to the opera "Faust," and I loved that one too.

One winter night as always, I was sharing the bed with Zoli and father covered us up. I said to him "Apúka hideg van és fázunk" (daddy it is freezing and we are cold), for which he replied "kezdjetek fingani" (start passing gas), and with that he kissed us both and left the room.

Soon, that bedroom was transformed into a working place for our parents. Since mother was a seamstress, she was working for a clothing business out of our apartment. Father was acting as a tailor, and with the use of patterns he was cutting fabrics to be sewed by mother. Father decided that he should take different clothing items to the *vására* (market) outside of the city of Budapest to make money. Suddenly, instead making of dresses, men's shirts were produced at our home. Father's sister, Eta, was traveling in from Rákoscsaba every day to help with the operation. I visualize clearly our mother and our aunt bent over the sewing machine, working extremely hard, pedaling away hour after hour. It seemed to me that mother was at the machine when we children went to bed and she was at it when we woke up.

Every day after school part of my job was to iron and fold those shirts, getting them ready for the market. Besides shirts, father was also selling pants, coats, and complete suits to the farmers. I can hardly imagine a harder job than going on the train day after day, visiting different towns, setting up tents early in the morning in rain, snow, or sunshine to be ready for the first customer; not an ideal situation. But that didn't bother our dad, at least he never complained, for he had a major responsibility to his family. Sometimes the market was good and sometimes it was terrible.

One day the communists took away all of that little business our parents created and father was crushed. Slowly, World War II, the Nazis, and finally the Communists were getting to him and according to mother (as she told me), Father almost committed suicide! He was gradually cracking up, which pretty much explains his fiery temper. Both of our parents must have gone through some incredible hardships and stresses in their lives.

One summer in the late 1960s I flew back to Boston to help him with his painting business. Teachers have the summer off; I needed work so I could augment my income (teacher's salaries were pretty low those days and still are). Actually, it was he who gave me a chance to make some money. This was the time when Edward Kennedy drove his car into the water, killing his lady companion in the process, while he saved himself from drowning by swimming to the shore. Father made the comment that nothing would happen to Teddy Kennedy because of his name and the great amount of money the Kennedy family has. I made the statement that in the United States everybody is innocent until found guilty. For this he came back with his famous comment: "Édes fiam, azért mert egyetemet végeztél még mindég olyan hüje vagy mint a fasz!"

Under Nazi and Soviet Rule

(My dear son, just because you went to college you are still as stupid as a dick.) When he said that I was furious at him, but as years went by I realized how right that statement is. Being a teacher and hanging around with college-educated people throughout the years, I have come across many dummies. Most of them have absolutely no common sense, although they have the book knowledge. It amazes me how dumb some of these people are. By the way, Ted Kennedy was acquitted of the murder charges just as father predicted it.

As a former classroom teacher I have talked a lot to my students about my upbringing, and life in Europe during the war, so that they may appreciate the life they enjoy in the United States. This also goes for the audiences at the Arizona Symphonic Winds concerts, for I close all of our concerts with the arrangement of "America The Beautiful." I always use my parents as examples, for because of them we all survived some of the most difficult times. They provided us children with unconditional love, wisdom, and values. Because of their examples we are hard workers, good human beings, good productive citizens, and contributors to the society in many ways, and we brothers have great love for each other.

2

Soccer Years

My teenage years

My basic education in Hungary consisted of the required eighth-grade schooling. While in the eighth grade we were given an exam to find out who was capable of handling higher education. I scored high enough for a continuing education, but my father wanted me to learn a trade. His philosophy was that all children should learn a trade first, and then further education may continue if one wants to pursue it. Since we had a large family, the family needed our monetary contribution to ease the burden on him and on our mother; however, the money part was very much in the secondary picture. Having a trade was the highest of importance for survival and success in life.

I went to a trade school and became an auto mechanic. At first I was upset about my father's decision in denying my higher education. However, without knowing the course of destiny, being a mechanic was a lifesaver for me. Two years of schooling was required to get a diploma. Every week was divided into two parts: we spent Mondays, Tuesdays, and Wednesdays in the classroom, and Thursdays, Fridays, and Saturdays at the factory. At the factory we were assigned to different stations for three-to-four month periods. At one station we worked on brakes only; at the next one on certain parts of an engine and so on. Each station had a highly qualified teacher and we had to pass a proficiency test before we were allowed to move to the next one. While in the classroom we had to wear uniforms with hats, like soldiers. In the beginning I was embarrassed to be seen in uniform by my friends but I got used to it. As a matter of fact, I enjoyed learning the trade I was involved in. The final exam at the factory was based on troubleshooting. We were driven out to an open field where a car was waiting for us. The object of the test was to put the car back into running condition and be able to drive it back to the factory. The purpose was simple; one should be able to take the vehicle back to the garage under any condition. Deliberately, traps were set and we had to find them. In one instance the brake pedal was going all the way down to the floor. We had to find the problem and fix it. A car should not be driven without brakes. Engine problems had to be taken care of; timing had to be adjusted by ear; also carburetors, for the correct mixture of gasoline and air; broken lines had to be taken care of; cut wires had to be found and mended, etc. The intentionally-created problems went on and on. All this had to be done with only the help of a screwdriver, pliers, and some wrenches, without the help of any outside diagnostic machines.

In May 1953, a month before my sixteenth birthday, I graduated as a certified automobile mechanic and within a few days I started to work at an automobile plant that was overhauling diesel trucks and diesel passenger buses, earning good income. My monetary contribution was a big help for the family.

Soccer playing years

At the same time, I was also involved with soccer and had played for a club outside of school since the age of eleven or twelve.

No Regrets

I was good at soccer, and at the age of eighteen I was selected to the All-Hungarian team, one step below the professionals. I remember clearly the day when I received my invitation for the All-Star training camp. We had a home game on a Sunday morning in late November 1955. The day was cold, extremely windy, and combination of rain/snow was falling. There was no audience present except for our coach and a man I had never seen before. He wore a raincoat with the collar turned up with one of his hands in his pocket for warmth while the other hand was hanging on to his hat. I couldn't see his face. As always, I was hustling and was playing an exceptionally good game under miserable weather conditions. We were glad when the game was over and had a chance to warm up next to the stove. Luckily that day we had warm water to shower with. On the way out from the clubhouse my coach pulled me aside and told me that the coach of the national team was scouting the game and he was very impressed with my playing. He extended his invitation for me to join the training camp in early spring for a possible selection on the national team!

The training camp was about forty miles outside of Budapest, in a beautiful area where all the top Hungarian athletes were preparing for the 1956 Olympic games. We trained very hard and at the same time were fed well, under great living conditions. During free time we had a chance to observe the track-and-field athletes. One afternoon I was present when the 4x1,500-meter runners set an unofficial world record. A few weeks later at an international competition they established an official new world record. At the training camp I won my position as left fullback on the National Team. I was elated, however at home my parents were not as carried away with the news as I was, or as was my older brother Zoli, who was glad for my accomplishment.

During practice a few days before my first soccer game as a member of the National Team I received a kick in my upper thigh, severely damaging muscle tissues. I didn't feel any pain while I was moving around, but as soon as the muscles cooled off I could hardly walk. I was hiding from my coaches; I did not want them seeing me limping, fearing that I might be dismissed from the team. Next day I went to one of the many famous Turkish baths in Budapest to soak my legs in the therapeutic mineral waters, followed by a massage to ease the pain. As the muscles cooled off the crusading pain returned. I had a difficult time walking but wanted to play the game more than anything. On the day of the game I got to the dressing room way before the coaches and slowly I started to warm up. By the time the coaches and the rest of the team arrived I was able to walk without a limp, although it was very difficult. The pain was there but I was hiding it.

It was time for us to line up in the stadium's tunnel to run unto the field in front of 100,000 people. Just as I looked up to the electronic scoreboard the name Veres was listed with huge letters in the lineup. I was excited, happy, and sad at the same time, wishing my parents could see me to share my elation and accomplishment. As we were taking the playing field I totally forgot about the pain; I felt as light as a feather flying gently in the breeze. As I remember, I played a good game and was congratulated by the coaches. I had a goal-line save, causing a great roar of approval from the fans in attendance. Zoli reminded me that he was at the game that day, and every time I did a good play he bragged to everybody around him, "That's my brother, that's my brother!" However, as soon as I made a mistake he kept his mouth shut.

After one of the practice sessions my coach approached me with an older-looking gentleman at his side. The stranger was a sculptor and was telling me that he was working on a statue and wanted to use me as a model, for in his opinion I had the best-looking leg muscles for his project. The finished product was to be erected at a soccer stadium somewhere outside of Budapest. He also told me that he would pay for my posing. Next day I went to his studio and sure enough there was a seven-meter (about twenty-one feet) sculpture of a soccer player in motion ready to kick the ball standing on a pedestal. It was a finished product; the only thing left to do was shaping of the leg muscles in movement. I did one hour of sitting on three different days, each time flexing separate parts of my leg muscles. By using soft plaster he was molding even the smallest of details. The finished creation was on display at the Fine Arts Museum in Budapest a few months later and my parents and I went to see it. By this time it was in bronze and looked very impressive. I wish I knew the name of the stadium and the city where it now stands. In 2001 Frances and I went to the Hungarian National Soccer League Headquarters in Budapest, hoping for someone who could help us find the place. No such luck. After all, this took place almost a half-century ago.

Before long I had a dilemma that had to be taken care of. I was doing well both in soccer and music at the same time and a decision had to be made about what direction should I be aiming for. I asked my mother for her opinion on this matter and her reply was quick and to the point, "…in sport by the time you reach the age of thirty or thirty-five you will be an old man, while in music you still will be young at age of sixty-five or seventy." Thanks to my mother's advice the predicament was settled once and for all.

While my parents never attended any of my soccer games, seldom did they miss my clarinet performances in Budapest; while in the United States they would travel thousands of miles to visit and see me teach in Tombstone; witness my high school marching band at the University of Arizona Band Day competition, and share the pride and joy with me as the top rating was awarded to me and my band; hear me play my clarinet with the Arizona Opera Company Orchestra, and see me conduct the Philharmonia Orchestra of Tucson in concert. I remember the opera that was performed when they were in town. It was Mozart's "Marriage of Figaro" at the Tucson Convention Center Music Hall. Linda, my wife at the time, was part of the cast singing the role of Susanna. During intermissions my parents would walk down to the orchestra pit looking down at the musicians. I didn't notice them until I heard my father's voice calling my name. I looked up and their faces told the whole story. They were the proudest parents and were sharing in the delight of my long time of study and final success. Years before they bought me a luxurious clarinet under the most difficult conditions in Hungary, provided private tutoring for learning, while I did the hard work. Very possibly for the first time we were on the same wavelength, sharing each other's accomplishments with great pride. Since I'm a parent myself and father of three boys, I hardly ever miss their performances, whether it is football, track-and-field, cooking, singing with the boy's chorus, marching band, concert band, or solo performances. I take great pride sharing in their achievements.

I had a very promising future in soccer; however, the Hungarian Revolution of 1956 interrupted it. I always played for a team called MTK, since the day I decided to play organized soccer. I started with lowest entry level, designed for eleven- or twelve year-olds. This same team was moving up to higher age group competition as the years went by. The team I played on went undefeated and was league champion year after year in their successive age groups. We were the envy of the opposing teams and their faithful fans. They loved us and hated us at the same time. They hated us because we beat them; on the other hand they admired us for the classic style of playing we exhibited. Many times the opposing fans were on our side because of the type of playing we put on display on the field. Our coaches were drilling the basics into us and were demanding team play with 100 percent dedication.

Even when injured I would finish playing the game. In one instance, I tried to block a kick with my right foot. The opposing team's player missed the ball but not my right foot, which he kicked with tremendous force. The impact made me lose my balance; I lost my footing and spun around, landing on my left arm. After getting up I noticed the swelling on my left wrist. During halftime the trainer put an Ace bandage around it and told me to see a doctor the following day. I finished playing the rest of the game not realizing that my arm was broken. I had a cast on it for six to eight weeks, still never missing a single game. That was my decision, not the coaches'.

I'm grateful for the discipline that was enforced and required from us youngsters. Being on a winning team required tremendous commitment and extremely hard work from every one of us, but it was well worth it. I learned at an early age that hard work would produce positive results. Later in life I incorporated this philosophy into my teaching career, and I try to believe this helped me to become a successful teacher.

Championship team in 1952, László holding the trophy.

The American/Hungarian soccer team in 1958. László is at far left.

3

The Lure of Music

The beginning of my musical career

My older brother Zoltán had friends who played musical instruments and formed their own band. This group would perform on different occasions and my brother would sing with that group. He was a great admirer of the great clarinetists Benny Goodman and Buddy DeFranco, and decided to learn to play that instrument. After a month of listening to the squeaking sounds he was producing, I expressed my desire and interest to learn the same instrument to my father. I told him that I could squeak and squawk just as well as my brother and with that, at the age of sixteen, my clarinet-playing career began. My parents were very supportive of us learning a musical instrument and eventually all of the brothers did the same.

Father had an old violin stashed away in a closet and at times he would play some simple tunes for us children. He must have played it fairly well because according to Zoli, in his younger years he played in a small band and they were available to play at dances or performing serenades under ladies' windows on hire. He was hoping that one of us boys would play that instrument but none of us had the desire to fulfill his wishes. At the time clarinet was more interesting to Zoli and me.

Our first teacher was a Mr. Gyarmaty, a member of the Hungarian Postal Service Wind Band. He would come to our house to give us lessons. One day he handed a book to me to read and said, "You will enjoy the story." The book was about the life of Verdi, the great Italian opera composer. I got into the book and couldn't put it down. The life of that man had a great influence on me in the field of music. That book introduced me to the wonderful world of opera and got me excited about learning to play the clarinet.

It was decided that we should enter the music school for more serious study. While Mr. Gyarmaty was a nice man we needed to move on. Ferenc Baritz became our tutor at the music school. He was a fine teacher and fine player. I don't exactly recall how long Zoli stayed with him or when he took his lessons, for we were on different work schedules. I took lessons twice a week at the music school right after soccer practice. I guess I had a natural talent for that instrument as I was progressing well.

One day I asked Zoli to play a duet with me and to my surprise he agreed. It was something by Mozart and I was truly enjoying the first few measures when suddenly he walked away from the music stand. Situating himself front of a large mirror he started to improvise on the Mozart theme, emulating Benny Goodman with his clarinet being angled high toward the ceiling. I was upset and never asked him to play duets with me again. Actually, he looked good in front of the mirror and was doing a good imitation of his idols. I always thought that Zoli was talented, had good technical facilities and a good feel for jazz.

At the end of the first year we students had to perform in a recital. I remember being part of a duet with a cellist. Zoli told me recently that I was also playing something by myself on the recital and the teacher told Zoli that he should do his performing first because it would be embarrassing to follow me with his playing. I

The Lure of Music

don't remember that, but Zoli told me that he would remember his teacher's words forever. We both had a good laugh.

First recital, age 17

Holding an Albert system clarinet at age 18

Béla Bartók Conservatory of Music

After two years of study I had to perform in front of a panel of adjudicators. One of the adjudicators from the panel suggested that I should take an audition at the Béla Bartók Conservatory of Music in the summer. The year was 1956. My father bought a brand new Boehm system clarinet for me for this great honor. Up until that point I was playing on the Albert system, which is totally different from the Boehm system. In August of that year I went to my audition without knowing what to expect. In the warm-up room there were about sixty to eighty clarinet players warming up, playing at a much higher level than me. I felt intimidated but went into a corner and did a very basic warm-up. I had a very simple solo prepared and as far as scales were concerned, I had difficulty playing them for I was just getting used to the new clarinet system.

It was my turn to play in front of a panel of jurors. I recognized one of the judges, for he was the one who suggested my auditioning. One of the jurors asked me for a certain scale to which I replied that since I have just changed over to a new system of fingering I wasn't sure if I could play it. However I did tell them that I could play the E major scale, which I did for three octaves. After that I played my short, simple solo. Results were to be posted in a few days. I continued with my daily routine, which consisted of working as an automobile mechanic in a factory from 7:30 A.M. until 4:30 P.M., followed with soccer practice and twice a week with clarinet lessons. In those days I did not get home until about 10:00 P.M. Streetcars were my mode of transportation.

Days went by since my audition and I had forgotten about it, totally knowing that I did not stand a chance. My father took a break from his work and showed up at the Music Academy to find out the audition results. Here is his report to my mother and me and possibly to Zoli: "I was in my overalls, working clothes, and while standing there one of the administrators approached me telling me that the school had no need for anyone to work on the large

The Lure of Music

heating stove at this time. Standing way back from the bulletin board a bunch of students were gathering and talking among themselves, asking each other, 'Who is László Veres?' I just stood there, not saying a word and finally, slowly moved myself closer to the bulletin board. On the board only one name was listed and that was Laci's. Our son was the only person who was accepted as a student. I started to cry and without muttering a word, slowly walked out of the building feeling an incredible pride inside of me."

My clarinet teacher at the conservatory was Professor Károly Váczi. He was a fine taskmaster with great emphasis on details. He emphasized the importance of long notes and how to connect those notes the smoothest possible way while producing a beautiful sound. Not even the smallest mistake on my playing part would escape his attention. He wasn't familiar at all with the new Boehm system clarinets and felt uncomfortable with it, but still he was a very fine teacher. I also had to take lessons on the piano. I remember well my piano teacher's comment to me one day: "You have a very gentle touch on the keyboard."

My studies at the music academy did not last long for the Hungarian Uprising of 1956 interrupted it. Sorry to say, today my piano playing is non-existent. Two months into the 1956-57 school year on Tuesday, October 23, my life took an unexpected turn and moved the course of my destiny into a direction of which I would never have dreamed. The turn of the events changed not just the life of my family, but also the lives of millions.

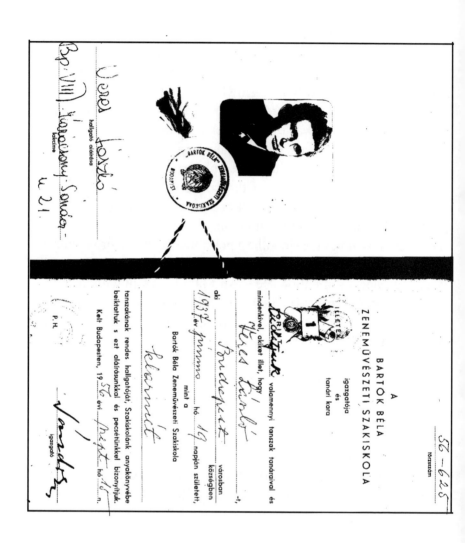

*Admission certificate to the
Béla Bartók Conservatory of Music*

4

Hungary Revolts

The Hungarian Uprising of 1956

Stalin, the Soviet dictator, died on Thursday, March 5, 1953. Zoli reminded me that on that day all sirens in Budapest were turned on, bringing the city to a total standstill. We were informed that comrade Stalin passed away and it was time to give homage to the great "father" of our country. The public was also informed that one had to stand in silence until the sirens were completely turned off. Zoli also reminded me that our grandmother on Father's side had a tremendous hatred toward Stalin. She died of cancer a few months before him, losing out on the pleasure of seeing him go first.

After the death of Stalin, Nikita Khruschev became the new leader of the Soviet Communist Party. In February 1956 Khruschev, in his "secret speech" to the Twentieth Party Congress of the Soviet Communist Party, denounced the Stalin doctrine and exposed him as a murderer of millions of people. The party's chiefs decided that power was to be taken away from any one dictator and moved over into the hands of the party leaders. By that time, virtually every country in the communist block was in confusion caused largely by the uncertainty of the situation, whether the "destalinization" was meant to nullify Stalin's policies or just simply to dress them up in new clothing. These unstable circumstances led to turmoil in Poland first, followed by, in a few months, the Hungarian people's peaceful demonstration, ultimately leading up to the Hungarian Revolution of 1956.

While in the sixth, seventh, and eight grades, every so often we were required to wear a white shirt with a red bandana around our necks held in place by a wooden ring. We students were the pioneers. In this uniform we marched every year during the May 1st parade held at *Hosok Tere* (Heroes Square). As we marched by the reviewing stand in front of all the communist party leaders, we were told to wave our hands, smile at our leaders, and at the same time yell, "Éljen Rákosi!" (Viva Rákosi! Mátyás Rákosi was the much-hated leader of the Hungarian Communist Party, a puppet figure picked for the position by the Kremlin in Moscow.) Across from the reviewing stage on the wide boulevard stood the huge bronze statue of Stalin. During the eve of the 1956 uprising the statue was toppled over by the freedom fighters and spat on by thousands.

I didn't mind the parade; most of us kids were looking forward to it, knowing that after the march we had a chance to spend the whole afternoon in the city's amusement park, called Város Liget.

Zoli also refreshed my memory by telling me that two of our younger brothers, George and Stephen, who were in first and third grades respectively, were regularly told by their teachers to question their parents as to why they were not members of the communist party. Father's response was a constant, "I'm working on it, maybe next week." He wasn't about to join; he hated Stalin, Rákosi, and the communist party as much as our grandmother did, possibly even more. The party that wanted him to join took away everything from my parents, causing Father to almost commit suicide.

Hungary Revolts

After being in the United States for a few years, one day I asked my father, "Do you ever have the urgent desire to return to Hungary? Are you ever homesick?" He had anger in his voice when he finally replied, "The only thing that blank, blank country ever did for me is to make my life and my family's life most miserable. I don't miss the constant living in fear and secrecy, never knowing when the Nazi Gestapo or the Communist's AVO (secret police) might knock on the door during the night, dragging the whole family or me away." I felt terrible for him and a great sadness took hold of me. Possibly for the first time I realized the depressed conditions he and mother lived under in the old country. Interestingly enough, many years later I posed the same question to my mother and except for the "blanks" her answer was much the same.

The day was October 23, 1956. It was a Tuesday and for me it started out like any other day: work at the automobile factory, studies at the conservatory, and soccer practice. A typical day for me was from about 6:00 A.M. until 10:00 P.M. every day but Saturdays and Sundays. Saturdays I just worked and Sundays were used up by soccer games only. On that Tuesday after work I was on my way to the conservatory for my classes, riding the streetcar as always. The mood on the streetcar was different from any regular days. People were talking about a demonstration that was taking place somewhere in the city. I was listening but did not pay serious attention to the talking that was going on. When I approached the conservatory the door was closed and a notice was taped on the door: "Today's classes are cancelled due to a public demonstration." That was the last time I saw the conservatory building until 1998, forty-two years later, when I went back to visit my homeland.

I followed the people as they were gathering, tagging along with them to Petőfi Sándor Square. There were some speeches given, but because of the size of the crowd and the noise around each other it was difficult to hear. The size of the demonstrators was growing in numbers and very quickly the square was overflowing. Most of them were very excited about the speeches and there was a constant yelling in unison: "Éljen a Magyar!" (Long live the Hungarians!) It was a peaceful demonstration. One of the speakers suggested that we all should go to the Budapest Radio Station located on Bródy Sándor Street.

The demonstrators wanted to broadcast their demands on the radio for all the people in Hungary to hear. Some of the demands were: removal of the Soviet Army from all of Hungary; removal of the Kremlin-controlled Hungarian puppet government; return former premier Imre Nagy into leadership position; better living conditions for all; freedom of speech and press; multi-party system; and removal of the feared AVO secret police. While the demonstration went on, more and more people were gathering, numbering to the estimate of 150,000. Erno Gero, recently appointed first secretary of the Communist Party, made a broadcast on the radio that quickly changed the mood of the people. He accused the demonstrators as enemies of the people and would not consider any of their demands. He intimidated them with arrests unless immediately dispersed. Gerö's threatening speech added fuel to the fire.

Suddenly gunshots were heard and panic set in. Tear gas was thrown at the demonstrators to disperse the crowd. The stampede began and people were on top of each other. Being in good physical condition luckily I did not get hurt, although, I came very close to receiving serious physical injury. People were screaming at top of their voices, bodies all around were being stepped on. It was a total mess.

I walked home the distance of several miles and it was around 11:00 P.M. when I reached our apartment complex. My parents were waiting up for me, of course worried, for they had no clue what events were taking place in the inner city. They had received plenty of rumors especially through the radio. I told my parents what had happened and went to bed. Gunshots from the distance woke me up between 3:00 and 3:30 A.M. These gunshots were becoming more and more frequent and louder and louder. This was an unusual event for me, for although I had heard gunshots before, these were different. Even during WW II it was mainly the explosion of the bombs we heard and not the rapid, steady gunfire. I knew that this was most likely caused by the demonstration that took place the night before. My father was already up and was listening to the radio broadcast. The announcer was advising people to stay in their homes and not to go to work, for there was dangerous fighting taking place on the streets of Budapest.

My parents were worried mainly because of my older brother Zoltán. In Hungary at the age of twenty, all men were being drafted into the military to serve for two years. After basic training the solders were assigned to one of the many different branches of the military. My brother was assigned to the AVO division, the much-hated secret service feared by the people. Since he played a musical instrument (clarinet), he with others organized a band and had a good life while fulfilling his military obligations.

Listening to the radio in the early hours, we found out that the Hungarian military was called in to control the demonstrators, which eventually led to an uprising against the government. Since my brother was stationed in the city of Budapest, we were definitely sure that Zoli had to be among the soldiers who were called in by the government to help put down what started out to be a peaceful protest.

As I look back many years later to the events that took place, I can understand the worry of my parents. My mother worries about anything when her child is concerned, while my father's thinking process involves common sense reasoning that eventually leads to worry. One has to understand the circumstances that were taking place in such a short time. World War II was barely over (1945). During that war the Jewish problem was a major worry for my father to protect his family from the Nazis, and to survive in those most difficult times; and now, a little over a decade later (1956), his son is serving his military obligation in the hated AVO and fighting against his own countrymen in the revolution. The worry escalated when the radio broadcaster announced that the revolution by the people was successful, for many of the soldiers refused to fight against their own. When a soldier refuses to fight or disobeys orders, the ranking officer will shoot the soldier on the spot without asking questions.

A few days later we found out that Zoli was among the many who disobeyed orders and was in hiding not from the officers anymore, but from the people of the revolution who were carrying guns. These people were chasing down AVO personnel and when captured, killing them in many different ways, the most popular being hanging. Most high-ranking AVO officers were hanged from a tree branch by their feet, while people stabbed them and whipped them, giving them the same type of torture that they had administered on many innocent people in the past. It was a slow, tortuous death. They were hung totally nude from the waist up, body parts cut out or down, blood everywhere on their bodies. The sight of these people was most grotesque. They were left there for a long time for the people to see.

AVO, the Hungarian Secret Police

The Hungarian AVO was a carbon copy of the Soviet KGB established by Stalin. It was a killing machine and people trembled when the AVO showed up at their doorstep. Once the AVO took someone away, very few ever saw the sunlight again. They simply disappeared without any trace. At the time I did not know those facts, but later from much reading I found out what Stalin's killing machine was capable of. The main AVO headquarters where these tortures took place was on Andrassy Blvd. in Budapest close to the Danube River. When the revolutionaries took over that place to release some of the prisoners and capture AVO personnel, they found a huge meat grinder under ground that emptied into the river. That was what happened to many who were taken away by the

Hungary Revolts

AVO. After elongated, unbearable torture they were thrown into the grinder.

I did not know any of these things, but my father did. Now one can understand the incredible fear my parents lived through. They raised five boys in the most difficult circumstances. It is easy to understand years later why politics were never discussed among the family, why everything was hushed, and why my father listened to the Radio Free Europe broadcast so softly that his ears were right next to the speakers, scared to death that someone might overhear it and turn him in. People were turning each other in for their own advancement in their jobs or for reward money. Friends did not trust each other. That was Stalin's way of controlling his people. The German Nazis used the same method during the Jewish roundup during the war. They offered reward money to people for turning Jews in. Especially in Poland the greedy people turned in innocent Jews for the small ransom money, but so did other countries. That is what happened to Anne Frank and her family in Amsterdam. A close friend of the family collected some money for this God-awful act.

The Hungarian AVO was a merciless agency. From reading later in life I found out a few things passed down by the few survivors. In one instance, a concert violinist was called in to the captain's office and was asked to play his violin. He had to stand all the time and no water or bathroom breaks were given. After fourteen hours of non-stop playing, he finally collapsed. The AVO man broke his violin into pieces, and with a hammer broke every single bone in all of his fingers then sent him back to his cell. Another incident: people were asked to face the wall and hold up a pencil that was placed between the wall and their foreheads with the sharp, pointed end facing the skin. They were told that if the pencil dropped they would be shot like dogs. They stood there for hours. In some instances the pencil was dropped and they were shot. There were instances where the pencil's sharp point went through the skin and embedded into the skull about an inch deep.

No Regrets

When I was in the *lager* in Graz, Austria (*lager* was the name given for the temporary holding place for us refugees), I met a woman who was about forty years old. This woman was always wearing white gloves on her hands. As I recall, she was very attractive and a very friendly person. One day during dinner I was sitting across the table from her and asked why she wore those gloves all the time. My curiosity was answered. She took off her gloves and showed me her fingers. All of her fingernails had been pulled out one by one by the AVO just a few months earlier. She had no idea why the AVO got hold of her. Another person in the *lager* had a big, burned hole in the palm of his hand. He had to hold his hand above a burning candle for hours while he was questioned by the AVO.

Rescuing Zoli

The date was about October 28, the uprising was victorious, and the Hungarian Army refused to fight against its own people. Mainly the Soviet soldiers who were stationed in Hungary did the fighting and they were defeated.

Somehow my father found out where Zoli was hiding. Zoli had his AVO uniform on, and didn't dare to go out to the streets for as soon as someone recognized the uniform, Zoli would be a dead person. The youngsters who were carrying rifles didn't know (the same held true for adults also) that except for the AVO officers, these soldiers were drafted and serving their military obligations.

My father called me and told me to go along with him to rescue Zoli. I remember the event as if it had happened yesterday.

Father and I took off walking. He was wearing a trench-type overcoat and so was I, as it was late October. We walked on Karácsony Sándor Street, and then turned left on Népszinház Street. We walked towards the inner city until we reached Nagy Körút Blvd., where we turned left. The sight was unbelievable. Blown up Russian tanks were scattered all over this beautiful boulevard,

Hungary Revolts

and human bodies laid everywhere. Some were burned beyond recognition. Some bodies were blown to pieces, a head here, an arm and a leg there, intestines scattered all over the place. We were stepping between these dead people and so were others, looking for their loved ones.

This sight went on for blocks until we arrived at our destination. I do not remember the name of the street, but we arrived at the address we were looking for. After climbing some steps we knocked on the apartment door. The door opened and the gentleman who stood there was no other than my father's old friend from the seminary and the same person who helped in changing all of us boys' birth certificates during the Nazi occupation.

Zoli was inside the apartment with his AVO uniform on. Father wore extra clothing on himself. Zoli changed clothing, however, we forgot to bring an extra pair of shoes with us. Father gave Zoli his own shoes, and he put on Zoli's military boots. A fire was built in the furnace and the uniform was thrown in it. We stood there watching the uniform dissolve into ashes. On the way home, my father took off his overcoat and tied it around his waist like an apron, covering the boots totally. If someone should have spotted him in those boots, it would have been sure death. We got home safely late at night for he did not want to walk during daylight for reasons mentioned. At home the first thing he did was light up the furnace and burn the boots. The windows had to stay open during the night to get rid of the smell.

That was the last time I saw Zoli until I arrived in Vienna on November 7, 1956. In the case of Zoli, he had no choice but to escape to the West to avoid being captured for refusing to carry out orders. He wasn't the only one; there were many others. The victory of the revolution lasted only a few days, for the Kremlin decided to send in a few divisions of their military forces to put an end to the uprising. This they did in no time, carrying out their orders mercilessly.

5

Hungary Repressed

The end of the short-lived, triumphant Hungarian uprising

The Soviet tanks were rolling in and covered the most dangerous parts of the city where the revolutionists were holding their positions. The freedom fighters put up a short resistance but were no match for the powerful Soviet Army. Curfew was established. If a sniper took aim at a Soviet tank from a building, the tank would point its barrel at the building and shell it. The tanks were ordered to shell any building for the smallest of suspicious activities. Needless to say, within a short time fewer snipers were to be found.

My father ordered all of us to take safety in the bomb shelter. Since we lived on the fourth floor of the apartment building, it took some time to descend the steps into the shelter. Since I was young and energetic, I was one of the last ones in the downward procession, making sure others got to safety first, especially children and elders. I was around the second floor, when a tremendous explosion with an incredibly loud sound took place. The noise was deafening and I know it damaged my ear for life. It was like a

Hungary Repressed

snap. The streets in Budapest are narrow; the tall buildings are next to each other creating an echo. This echo made the sound multiply many times over. With a damaged ear, I had no business going into the music field, which I did later on in life. The only other time I heard a loud noise like that was on the army base at Fort Huachuca. I was in the barracks and stepped outside to enjoy the cooling thunderstorm. At that point lightning hit the fifty-five-gallon oil barrel used as a trash can next to the barracks. The incredibly loud sound followed by the lightning caused still more damage to my ears.

The bomb shelter was full and my father and I settled into one of the empty apartments on the first floor away from the main entrance of the building. It was getting late and it was very cold. My father found a few pieces of newspaper and put them on the floor. That was to be our mattress and blanket for the freezing night. I lay down on the cold floor, shivering, but somehow managed to fall asleep. Early the next morning I was awakened by my father and others, for they were seeing smoke coming out of our apartment and were screaming, "Fire, fire!" My father and I ran upstairs and found the pillow on my bed totally ablaze, spreading the fire to the mattress and other parts of the bed's wooden frame. We were lucky to catch the fire in its early stages and we managed to put it out. After calming down we noticed a bullet hole in the wall. I was lucky. If we had stayed in our apartment that night instead of in that icebox apartment on the first floor, I would not be here writing about it. Someone was watching over the family and me.

The Soviet Army had no trouble putting an end to the short-lived, but heroic Hungarian Revolution of 1956. The rumor was that more and more Hungarians were fleeing the country. We knew that Zoli had escaped to Vienna, for somehow he sent a message through Radio Free Europe with a fake name.

The radio station in Budapest was under the communist's control again and was broadcasting their typical propaganda.

No Regrets

The people of the uprising were called dirty, filthy people, nothing but a mob who tried to overthrow the well-established peace-loving government and our friends from the Soviet Union who had to come in to establish peace again. They were encouraging workers to get back to their jobs, although the transportation system was pretty much at a standstill. Somehow I got to my work place but the factory wasn't opened. I got home early, around 10:00 A.M., and my father was waiting for me anxiously. He told me to put myself together in a hurry for I was going someplace. I put on my worn out, faded warm-up uniform from the soccer club I played for and grabbed my new clarinet, purchased by my parents just a few months ago (I still have that instrument). He told me that most likely I wouldn't be coming back again.

    I barely had a chance to kiss my mother good-bye. We were hurriedly running down the steps and on the street as my father started to explain to me what was going on. The rumor was that the Soviets were gathering together young people of my age, for the Kremlin was blaming the uprising mainly on the young university students and some of their professors. I wasn't a university student, but my father didn't want to take a chance on me. He also told me that the collected people were to be shipped to Siberia. He said a truck was waiting at *Teleki Tér* (the playground where we youngsters grew up) to take me close to the Austrian border. He told me that if anybody asked where I was going, to tell him or her that I was going to visit a sick aunt at such and such a village (the name I don't remember). The playground was less than a half-mile away. I remember it was a clear, beautiful day, and the air had its typical early November bite. The sun had a bright shine, giving a feeling of well-being to the human body.

    The truck was standing there with the motor running. It was obviously a stolen military truck; it was covered with a dark green canvas all around, except for the back where it had a flapping opening. I saw my father giving a large amount of cash to the driver, and then he came over to me to give me the biggest and

Hungary Repressed

warmest hug I had ever received from him. There was sadness in his face and he was not able to hold back his tears. "Go, édes fiam (my sweet son), to the West to find yourself a better life. Your brother Zoli is already in Vienna, make sure you find him, and try to let us know somehow that you are alive and safe." He gave me the address of one of my uncle's brothers, a person I had never heard of before. His name was Jeno (Eugene). He and his wife had lived in Vienna since the 1930s. He told me that Jeno would be able to help me get in touch with Zoli. I memorized the address and still remember it. The house number escapes my memory, but the name of the street was Bartenstein Gasse.

I jumped in the back of the truck and both of us waved to each other. There was an incredible sadness on his face, a sight I shall never forget. He unselfishly let one of his beloved sons go into the totally unknown, not knowing if he, my mother, or my brothers would ever see me or hear from me again. I saw my father cry only once before and that was at his mother's funeral. This was different. Those tears were screaming at me, "I love you, édes fiam."

6

Fleeing the Iron Curtain

Escape from Hungary

At first my sadness did not kick in, for I was excited about the new adventure that was waiting for me. I looked around in the truck and noticed it for the first time that I wasn't alone. The fifteen or so people on the truck were quiet and looked scared. I recognized one of the couples for they were our next-door neighbors. They had their little girl with them and because she was born with some kind of back problems, she was wearing a cast on most of her upper body. She was a very pretty girl and was about six or seven years old. The others on the truck were strangers to me, although all of us had the same thing in common: to cross the border to Austria, and into the free world.

The truck was traveling toward southwest Hungary at first and then eventually straight to the West. Soldiers at checkpoints stopped us many times. They asked questions, and wanted to see our identification papers. I didn't have one on me and just told them that I was on my way to see my sick aunt. Each time they let us go, although some of the passengers were taken from the truck. I have no clue as to what happened to them. Needless to say, all of

Fleeing the Iron Curtain

us on the truck were scared. After traveling on the road again for about an hour the truck came to a sudden halt. Another checkpoint stop? Since I was the one sitting closest to the back of the truck next to the flap part of the canvas that covered the vehicle, I was expecting the flap to be opened by soldiers to point their flashlights into our faces. One tense, scary moment was taking place. I heard the driver's door open and close, but this time there was no talking outside as at previous checkpoint stops. The back flap opened and the only person standing there was the driver. He spoke to us in a subdued quiet voice: "This is as far as I can take you. Follow the road ahead of you, take a right turn at the dirt road (all roads were dirt), take a left, then a right, and you will find a small home with a barn next to it. Someone will be waiting for you and that person will give you directions toward the border."

We got off the truck. It was pitch dark, but at last my eyes were getting used to the darkness, and were able to see the road and pick out objects. By guessing, I was figuring the time to be around 6:00 P.M. The temperature was dropping and was getting colder by the minute. The date was November 6, 1956, and the cold winter was knocking on the door.

I found out later on that we were dropped off at the outskirts of the city called Szombathely, located in west-central Hungary, about twenty miles from the Austrian border.

We started our walk. As the youngest of the group (nineteen years old), I became the leader of the few of us who stayed with the group. I made sure to stay close to my neighbors in case the little girl in the cast needed help. We followed the driver's directions not knowing if he had sent us into the Soviet military or not. After walking for a long time, we arrived at our destination, and sure enough, an older man was waiting for us with a lantern in his hand. He led us into the barn and told us to lie down on the hay to re-energize our bodies, for there was a long journey waiting ahead of us. It felt good to lie on the hay totally stretched out. He told us he would be back later to give us directions. Now a second person had to be trusted. Is he going to turn us in or not? I was very sleepy, but stayed awake in case there was danger brewing around us, especially me. The adrenaline must had been flowing in full force inside of me, for I didn't even notice that I was hungry, thirsty, or tired.

The old man emerged as he said he would and told us it was time move on. We all got up and went outside. This time there was a little moonlight, not a good thing, for the border guards could spot us more easily. He told us which direction to go, which dirt road to follow and we were on our way; again I was leading the group of eight. The area was open farmland and since we were in the month of November, the land was barren, except for some trees here and there. We could hear the sound of the machine guns, and as we walked they became louder and louder. The sound of the guns told us that we were getting closer to the border. We also heard dog barks, but they were very distant, which made at least me feel better. The last thing I wanted to do was run into guard dogs.

We arrived at a small creek with water in it. I tried to force my eyes in the dark with the help of the very slight moonlight to find a bridge or to make a makeshift bridge for crossing. I could not find anything and decided to go into the water to get to the other side. Throwing a rock into the creek, I noticed that it wasn't very deep. The father of the little girl, Kövári Erno, asked me if I would carry their little girl across for I was stronger then he was. I told him I would and in exchange he would have to carry my clarinet. I told him to keep it above his head and to not let water get to it.

I picked up the girl and held the precious thing in my arms as we entered the ice-cold water. I got to the other side and Erno with his wife crossed a few minutes later. The girl was totally dry, but I was soaked. When they crossed I asked for my clarinet, and they told me that it was accidentally dropped in the water and it was still there. I was furious and went back to the creek looking

Fleeing the Iron Curtain

for my instrument. Luckily, I found it. I dropped on my knees and opened the case. I took off my warm-up jersey, the only dry clothing on me, and with it I dried my clarinet piece by piece, while cussing away in Hungarian. I didn't even notice the freezing cold air around me.

We kept walking without realizing that we were going uphill. All of a sudden on top of the hill I noticed lights in the distance. Immediately I told everybody that it had to be Austria, for in Hungary the smaller towns and villages had no electricity. Newly energized and with new hope, we increased our walking speed. The machine guns were still firing away but they were in the distance; however, the sound of the guard dogs was getting closer. I had only one thing on my mind: move ahead and make it to the other side. As much as I was angry at Erno for dropping my clarinet into the creek, I was still helping them along with their little girl.

As the lights from the other side were getting closer, suddenly I noticed smoothness in the ground and knew right away that we were in part of a land that belongs neither to Hungary nor Austria. We were crossing the border that was about as wide as half of a football field when I heard a voice calling from the short distance. "Commen sie heir, bitte," said the voice, over and over. I recognized the language being German and after a few more steps the men in uniform turned on their flashlights and with it indicated what direction we should continue. The men in uniform were the Austrian border guards patrolling the area. They could not put the flashlight on earlier, since we were still in the neutral zone, but as soon as we reached Austrian land they could do it. We waited for a while until the rest of the group got across also.

They led us farther into Austria's territory, where a smaller van was waiting. We got in and they took us to the temporary shelter set up by the International Red Cross. We found out that we were in the city of Graz, the second largest city in Austria, located about fifty miles from the Hungarian border. As we entered the

No Regrets

Red Cross shelter (*lager*) in the early hours of the next day, other refugees were already there. They handed me a cup of hot chocolate, my first drink and nourishment since I had left Budapest. It tasted marvelous. At the same time they passed out small tubes of toothpaste, toothbrushes, and some dry clothes. Brushing my teeth for the first time in many hours (days?) gave a freshness and cleanness to my mouth. They also had some sandwiches for us.

They took us into a makeshift room where some double bunk beds were put together for us to sleep on. They must have been built in a hurry, for they were not very strong. Two bunks were next to each other held together with a nail or two to increase the strength. I took one of the top bunks in the middle of the room. Burlap material filled with hay was our mattress. I stretched out and fell asleep on my back in no time. I was awakened from my deep sleep by feeling somebody's hand on my private part. I grabbed the hand that was touching me, picked it up in the air, and with all my might I slammed it on the top of this person's body. The bunk where this other person was collapsed, and he fell to the lower bunk. Luckily the lower bunk was empty at the time. This young man, who was about the same age as I was, in his embarrassment disappeared and I don't recall ever seeing him again.

The next day we walked outside our *lager* for a little sightseeing in the city. At one of the pubs I noticed a Coca-Cola sign. From the many books I had read back in Hungary, Coca-Cola seemed like a very popular drink in America and in the West. Curiosity got me into the pub. I wanted to taste it. We were told in the *lager* that the local merchants were willing to help the refugees as much as they could. I asked for a glass of Coke, anticipating the delicious taste of that much heard of drink. I took a few sips and spit it out. The bartender was laughed at me and so did the other patrons present. I said, "Danke shöne," and walked out. Once on the street, I could not believe that millions of people drink that awful tasting stuff. Forty-six years later I still don't drink Coca-Cola, or any other kind of soft drinks for that matter.

Fleeing the Iron Curtain

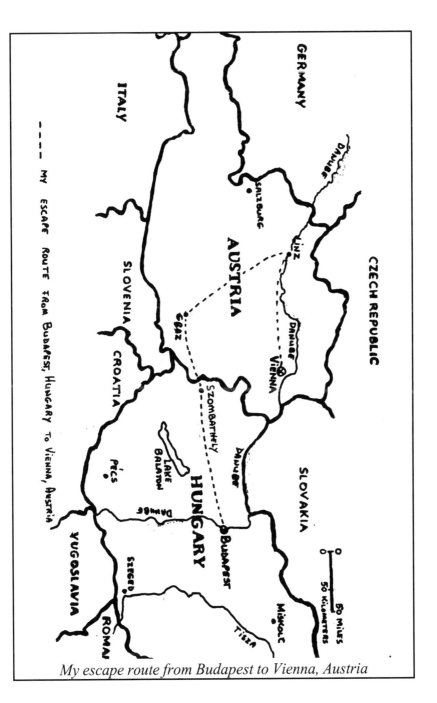

My escape route from Budapest to Vienna, Austria

7

To the Land of the Free

Looking for my brother, Zoltán

The Red Cross kept us in the *lager* for about two days for processing. I met some people there, including the woman who wore white gloves all the time, and another person with a hole burned into his palm, both carrying with them some of the Hungarian AVO's famous trademarks. However, as they would say, "We are glad to be alive."

In the early afternoon of November 8, the Red Cross people took us to the Graz Railroad Station where we boarded the train. Destination: Linz, Austria, about 100 miles northwest of Graz. Linz had a much larger *lager* for the Hungarian refugees, with more processing facilities and more available spaces for living accommodations. The *lager* was an old military base, re-opened for the Hungarian refugees. The city of Graz was kind enough to provide shelter for a few days for us escapees. By this time, I lost total contact with Ernö and his family. Years later I heard it from second hand that they eventually ended up in Argentina, where they had relatives. I often wonder whatever happened to that beautiful little girl in the cast.

To the Land of the Free

The train left the station in the late afternoon and darkness was settling in. I was pretty much by myself, for that is the way I wanted to be. Many things were on my mind: how was my family doing; how will I find Zoli and where; and what would the future hold for me. I wasn't afraid of the hardship and hard work that was waiting for me down the line. We were survivors and fighters.

Coming out of my dreams, I looked out the train window and the sight was incredible. The moon was out in its full splendor giving light to the magnificent countryside of Austria. I got up and walked to the back of the train and stood outside. The air was very cold but I didn't care. The train was crossing parts of the Alps. Snow-covered mountains surrounded us and small rivers were racing by. We entered many tunnels and every time we came out, it seemed like the new site was more beautiful then the previous one. While others were sleeping inside, I remained outside soaking in the picture postcard beauty of the countryside. We pulled in to the Linz station early the next afternoon.

We were taken directly to the *lager*. We entered the gate and marched to one of the buildings where bedding materials and military-type utensils were given us. We were told to go to the designated barracks, create our own cubicle, and settle down until dinnertime. However, I had other ideas. I walked to the front gate and talked to the guard on duty. I told him I had to go to Vienna as soon as possible. He told me that the highway leading to Vienna was not too far from the *lager*. All I would have to do is put my thumb out, he showed me how, and a car might pick me up if it's going in that direction. I thanked him, ran back to the barracks, and with my clarinet under my arm I walked toward the highway as darkness was slowly settling in. A sign was pointing in the direction to Vienna. The distance in kilometers was posted also, about 120 miles. There were no cars going by either direction when I got there. Suddenly a car came on my side of the road and I put my thumb out as the guard demonstrated it to me. The car slowed down and halted.

No Regrets

On my way to Wien (Vienna), Austria

    The driver of a Volkswagen van was a middle-aged man and in German asked me where I was headed. I didn't speak German, however I recognized some of the words and I understood his question. I told him in very broken German that would translate roughly as "I go Wien." He understood what I said and with his hand he signaled an invitation and pointed to the passenger seat. I took my seat and the van slowly started to roll, picking up speed on the highway. We had a one-sided conversation going on. As soon as he realized that I was one of the Hungarian refugees who couldn't speak German, he started to talk to me in Hungarian, which was awful, for I could not understand a word of it. To be nice, I was saying a bunch of "ja's" and my head was going up and down at the same time signifying that I understood him.
    At one point he asked me if I was hungry. I wasn't sure if that is what he said and while I was thinking about it, he was slowing the van down and pulled into a pub located off the highway. We went inside and he asked me again if I wanted to eat. I tried to be polite and somehow I managed to say, "No thank you." That was a big lie. I haven't eaten anything since we got on the train in Graz over thirty hours ago and I was starving. He ordered, and a few minutes later the waitress showed up with two huge ham and cheese sandwiches on large buns and two tall glasses of beer. He told me to "essen" (eat). First I refused, but eventually I threw away my pride for the hunger in me took over. I pretty much swallowed my sandwich and drank the full glass of beer. I felt much better and thanked him.
    We got in the van again and were on our way to Vienna. I had my uncle's cousin's address and he managed to find the narrow street with the right house number. Before I had a chance to thank him, he shoved a ten-shilling bank note into my hands. I thanked him again and told him "auf wiedersehen" (good-bye). The time was about 10:00 P.M. and I was in Vienna at the right

To the Land of the Free

address. I was happy as can be; it would only be a short time before I would get in touch with my brother Zoli.

The place was an apartment building and I walked up to the first floor and knocked on the door. There was no answer. I sat down on the steps and waited. It was Friday night, and I figured that my contact in Vienna was staying out with his wife having a good time someplace. Around midnight they showed up and I recognized him from pictures. He told me that Zoli was staying at Hundstum Platz and wrote it down for me. He told me to go downstairs, walk to the end of the street, and get on the streetcar at the corner. He also told me that the person who takes your ticket would tell you at what stop to get off. I thanked him and left. I never saw him again, and didn't want to see him again. I'll make more comments about this relative of mine at the end of this chapter.

Finding Zoli

I got on the streetcar around 12:30 A.M. There were many people on the streetcar on their way home, possibly from a late movie or opera or nightclub. Those days a person was covering the streetcars from one end to the other checking tickets or selling them. The ticket taker approached me and I told him, "Ich ein Ungarishe refugee" (I'm Hungarian refugee) and showed him the address I wanted to find. He tried to talk to me in German but we didn't get anywhere. The sign language at this time did not work. He told me to wait here and with that he walked toward the other end of the streetcar.

Finally he returned with a lady. I guessed her age to be in the fifties. She had a very friendly face with a gentle, caring smile. She spoke to me in Hungarian with a warm, soft voice. She told me that the ticket taker tried to look up the address in the book he carried with him, but was unable to find it. The address was simply not listed Vienna city's directory. She asked me why was I interested in that address. I told her that I had just arrived in Vienna and was looking for my brother who escaped from Hungary about ten days ago and was at that address. She told me that it was getting very late; nothing could be done at 1:00 A.M. and said, "Let me escort you to the police station where you can spend the night, and tomorrow morning I will come by and take you to the Red Cross, where they will able to tell us the exact location of your brother." I accepted her offer. She seemed sincere and caring.

    We got off at one of the stops and entered the police station. She talked to one of the policemen on duty in German. The policeman came over and led me to one of the cells. I waved goodbye to my rescuer as I was led away looking forward to some sleep, something I hadn't had for about forty hours. I was handed a blanket and he left the cell door open. There were other cells there occupied by others, however, their cells were locked. The cell had a wooden built-in bed slightly angled to keep the head on a higher level, acting as a pillow, for there was none. The wooden planks were my mattress. I didn't care, for I was dead tired. The only thing I remember after I laid down was somebody standing above me shaking me to get up. I could see the light outside and slowly I remembered where I was. My rescuer (from here on I'll call her my protective angel) was standing at the cell door. The new policeman on duty brought me some black coffee in a military canteen. My angel showed up as she said she would, telling me that it was time to go. It was about 9:00 A.M.

    Instead of going directly to the Red Cross she told me that she was going to take me to her apartment first to have something to eat. We walked to her apartment, which was not too far from the police station. It was a small apartment very nicely furnished, accented with many different sculptured figures and paintings. The large windows let the sunshine in, giving brightness and warmth to the rooms. She introduced me to her mother, who either lived there or was visiting, and we sat down to eat. It was a typical western continental breakfast with plenty of fresh rolls, butter, jam, and coffee. After talking for a while, I found out that she was an

To the Land of the Free

artist. Years later, as I met more artists in my life, I found them to be highly friendly and sensitive people.

We began our search for my brother. After taking a couple of streetcars, we arrived at the Red Cross. There were lots of people lining up on the street, all refugees like me. The sun was shining brightly; it was a beautiful November day. It was my turn to register, but this time in much more detail than at Graz. They wanted to know my exact date of entering Austria, my full name, previous address, etc. At the end they wrote down Zoli's address on a piece of paper and we were on our way. This time the address was spelled correctly, not like the last time as given to me by the so-called Hungarian connection. We had no trouble finding the location. We got on the streetcar, and after transferring a few times, we arrived. I thanked my angel many times and with that she left, and I was never to see her again. I never learned her name.

It was a dark brick building about four stories high and it reminded me of my elementary school building in Budapest. It had long hallways and from there classrooms opened both left and right. The bathroom was located in the middle part of the hallway for everyone to use. On the top floor at end of the hallway was the room where Zoli stayed with others. There were about eight beds in every room. The only empty bed was right next to the window and didn't take me much time to realize why that bed was empty. The window was broken and nobody wanted to enjoy the freezing cold breeze during the night or the cold rain or the snow, which was about to show up any day. The whole building had been changed into a temporary *lager* to house the Hungarian refugees, who were arriving day after day by the thousands. I truly appreciate the Austrian government and its people for sheltering us even if it was only temporary.

Zoli wasn't in the building at that time and I went downstairs and waited at the front door for him to show up. Time was going by and darkness was slowly settling in. I remembered the ten-shilling bank note in my pocket. (Ten shillings would equal about $2.00 in those days). There was a small dining place at the corner and I entered it. I sat down at the square table that was covered with a white cloth with some red color designs on it. When the waitress approached I took the money out of my pocket and put in on the table. I was making circular motions with one of my hands on my stomach, while my other hand imitating putting food into my mouth as I was telling her "essen" (eat). I was pointing with one of my fingers to the bank note. She got my message and left. Ten minutes later she returned with a full plate of food and a tall glass of beer. She took my money and returned with some change. On my plate was a huge piece of "Wienershnichle," lots of fried potatoes, and bread. I ate, drank the beer, and felt good.

I went back to the building again but still no sign of Zoli. Finally he showed up about 9:00 P.M., and we embraced and kissed each other. He told me that he was visiting this Austrian couple and they would like to meet me. I was to be introduced to them next evening. With that we went to bed. His bed was next to the door that was kept open to let some of the warm air in from the hallway. None of the rooms was heated, and on top of that ours had a broken window with my bed right next to it. I wasn't about to complain for I was about to sleep on an army bunk that had a mattress, sheets, pillow, and a blanket. It was more than I could ask for and I was more than thankful. I was in a free world and deep down I knew that a great future was waiting for me. I fell asleep and not even the cold air that was coming through the window bothered me.

Meeting the Weber family

Next day being Sunday, Zoli took me over to this Austrian family to meet. They lived across the square in one of the side streets. It was a very nice, typical European building kept in excellent condition.

We walked up the steps and I was introduced to Herr Otto

To the Land of the Free

Weber and his wife. These people were small in stature but big in heart. They welcomed me with open arms. They had a grown daughter Frida, but she had moved out years before and had a place of her own. We sat down to eat and since Otto spoke some Hungarian we were able to communicate, while everything had to be translated to his wife. Otto's mother or father was Hungarian. He was in his middle fifties and his wife was some years younger.

Zoli does not like to be tied down and be on somebody's schedule; he was happy that the Weber family liked me for he could be on his own doing whatever he wanted to do. The Webers had a nice overcoat waiting for me and they were very pleased that it was a perfect fit. They also got me a nice pair of shoes, shirts, pants, etc. In a short time I was a second child to them. They insisted that I come over for dinner every night and have lunch and dinner with them on weekends.

Frau Weber had a full-time job, while Otto was semi-retired. He helped me to get a job in a large diesel factory as a mechanic, a job I kept until it was time to go to the U.S.A. I was paid well for my work. My father's vision came true. "Learn a trade" was his motto and he insisted on that. He was right, for by having a trade in my hands I was able to get a well-paying job in a short time in a strange country.

Fridays were paydays. At the window where the money was issued we told the clerk our numbers. I called out with a strong voice, "dreihundert neun und fünfzig (359)," when it was my turn, and the cash was handed over (there were no checks given those days). I was excited and delighted about having my own money for the first time in a foreign country.

After work with money in my pocket I took the streetcar to downtown Vienna and did some shopping. In a few minutes I was the proud owner of my very first wristwatch. It was Swiss made "Doxa." I still have it and it still works. After that I walked over to one of the street vendors and bought myself a bag of beautiful oranges from Spain. I had never tasted an orange before in my life.

I sat down on the curb next to the vendor and ate all of the oranges, about ten of them, at one sitting. I was experiencing a totally different life, a life-style I never knew before except from the books I had read. At times I was wondering if it was only a dream. On my way home I picked up some flowers for Frau Weber.

Otto and Frau Weber, Vienna, 1956

I managed to save money; my parents taught me that. "There are always rainy days down the road, one has to prepare for them..." they used to say.

I saw Zoli only in the late evenings; he had his own agenda. I know that at one time he went back to Hungary, a dangerous undertaking, to encourage our parents to escape to the West. I understand that my father wasn't very happy when he showed up at the doorstep; as a matter of fact, he yelled at him for taking chances. The reason for his yelling at him had to be because when Zoli had been in the Hungarian Military—the hated AVO division—and had anybody recognized him, Zoli would have been a dead person and who knows who else with him. Zoli's encouragement must have helped, for in the early part of January 1957 my parents, three younger brothers, and my grandma left Budapest.

Years later Zoli told me that Father and Mother were slowly selling things to save money, money to be paid to the guides and drivers. My parents were also putting some valuable documents

To the Land of the Free

together to take along (birth certificates, pictures). Zoli in addition told me that father asked one of his sisters, who spent time with us often, to stay in the apartment until they were safe in Austria. My aunt Eta was seen by many of our neighbors in the past at our residence; she wasn't a stranger. Father played it safe; in case the escape turned out to be a failure, they had a home to get back to. There was a tremendous shortage of apartments those days, and empty apartments were given away fast.

Managing my life in Vienna

In Vienna I was busy working and having a good time. I went to the movies, did lots of sightseeing, and joined a small orchestra that was playing nothing but Viennese waltzes. I had a chance to play my clarinet again. The members of the group were very friendly, and made my stay most enjoyable while introducing me to the fine Austrian and German beers.

I kept close contact with the Webers and was a regular at their home. The only thing I did in the *lager* was sleep. By December and January, the cold air was really coming through the broken window even though I had it plugged with clothing material. I didn't care; it didn't bother me at all. I used my overcoat as an extra blanket, curled up into a position and stayed there until the alarm went off. I broke the world record when it came to dressing fast. There were no shower facilities in the *lager*, so I took my showers at the factory, or on weekends I would visit the "Bath Haus" for a nice hot shower. The price was minimal. The Webers didn't have a shower in their apartment either.

To get to my work place, I had to walk about a half-mile to the "Stadtbahn" (metro) and transfer to a streetcar that dropped me off at the factory. Coming home was more interesting. By 5:00 darkness covered the city and the countryside. Walking from the metro station after work, the street I had to walk on seemed to have different scenery than in the early morning hours. At first I didn't know, but soon found out, that part of the street I had to walk on was a red light district. I was invited by the streetwalkers almost every night; I tried to ignore them by increasing my walking speed. One night I built up my courage to ask one of them, "Wieviel?" (How much) She replied, "Fünf und zwanzig." (Twenty-five) I said, "Zuviel," (too much), and took off. I was never invited again.

A few months before the Hungarian Revolution I took a liking to the daughter of one of our neighbors. Her name was Györgyi (Georgia) and was about three years younger than I was. She was a very striking, beautiful girl, tall (slightly shorter than I), slender with long black hair. Because of my working schedule, not getting home until about 10:00 P.M. I didn't see her except on some weekends. My mother liked her a lot, for she was well-mannered, smart, and above all Jewish, for that was very important to my mother. One day I asked her if she would like to go to the movies with me. She said she would love to.

In late 1955 and early 1956 an Italian movie company was putting out full operas on film with great singers. I went to see many of them and enjoyed them tremendously. Some of them I saw more than once. The opera "La Traviata" by Verdi (my favorite opera composer) was playing downtown and I took her there. She loved it a lot and thanked me. We were holding hands and I'm not sure if it was my hand or hers, but one of us had a sweaty palm. We had a few more dates together until the revolution started. While in Vienna, using the Weber's address I started to write to her and she replied each time. The exchange of letters brought us closer, but the miles between us slowly separated us. When I came to the U.S.A. the correspondence slowly faded away. She was the first girl in my life I truly cared for. At times I wonder what ever happened to her.

One day I received news that the rest of my family had crossed the border and were in a *lager* in Kornebourg, about twenty miles outside of Vienna. On the weekend I took the train to visit

To the Land of the Free

them. It was good to see everybody. I remember spending Saturday and part of Sunday with them. We slept in the same room. My brothers were already sleeping and I was lying on the bed slowly dozing off, when my father asked me to talk about my escape. I told my story. When I came to the part in my narrative when I met my second uncle, I heard crying coming from both of my parents and my grandma.

Sunday afternoon I headed back to Vienna for work was waiting for me the next day. I gave most of my cash to my parents. This I did week after week, giving them all of my cash before I got on the airplane that took me to the U.S.A. The way I understood, Austrian currency couldn't be taken out of the country and since I was sponsored by the HIAS organization, my parents needed the money much more than I did.

Now comes my conclusion of my so-called contact, my uncle's brother in Vienna. This distant relative of mine didn't bother to ask if I was tired or hungry or even thirsty when he met me (remember that I was an alien to him). He and his wife let me out to a totally strange city in the middle of the night, knowing very well that I didn't speak the German language. A total stranger on the streetcar took me in and unselfishly offered her helping hand. The Weber family opened their home to me, helping me in my new surroundings. I guess this bothered my parents a lot more than it bothered me. By his not helping me, I became a stronger person along the way.

Getting ready to go to the United States of America

Austria was only a temporary refuge for us refugees. We had to move on to other countries. Many Hungarians returned to the homeland but most of them went on to pursue a new and different life. In Vienna, we had to register to a country that opened the doors for refugees. In South America, Brazil and Argentina opened their doors. In Europe, Sweden was willing to take some of us in; and in North America, Canada. I liked Sweden, however, I wanted to get out of Europe. We did register our names for Brazil (our parents and the rest of the family were still in Hungary at this time). A few weeks later news was spreading: the United States Congress passed a law opening up its quota to Hungarian refugees. The way I understand it, President Eisenhower had a great deal to do with this by putting pressure on the Congress. As soon as the rumor became real, we lined up to register for the U.S.A. It was a dream come true.

There was a big catch in getting to the U.S. Each person had to be sponsored by a family in the U.S. or some kind of religious organization. Being identified as Jewish, Zoli and I went to the HIAS organization (Hebrew Immigration Aid Society) to sign up. By this time our parents were in Austria. At the HIAS they wanted proof that we were Jewish. We had no papers for proof. In a moment, Zoli and I looked at each other and started to pull down our zippers. We were ready to drop our pants when the lady at the desk told us to stop. Proof was established. In the United States, it was a standard procedure to have every newborn boy circumcised in the hospital, unless the parents requested not to. In Europe, only Jewish boys were circumcised those days.

They took our names in the same order as we had registered weeks before at the Red Cross. Since Zoli had arrived in Austria ten days before I did, he also arrived in the U.S. that many days earlier than I. The rest of the Veres family landed in the U.S. three months later.

Going to the "Dream Land:" The United States of America

Zoli was already in the U.S. when I was called to report to a place where they kept us until departure. By this time I resigned from the factory, exchanged hugs with the Webers, and thanked them for everything they had done for me. For a while I kept up correspondence with them, but sorry to say, that also faded away,

To the Land of the Free

just as it did with the girl in Hungary. Otto Weber's knowledge of the Hungarian language was limited, especially when it came to writing, and my German was almost non-existent, which made corres- pondence very difficult. Many times I think of all of them with warm thoughts, wondering what ever happened to them.

I said good-bye to my family, knowing that in a few months we would hook up somehow, with the help of HIAS in the U.S. While at this temporary holding place, I lost all contact with my parents. I don't exactly remember how many days we spent there, but it wasn't for many. On the morning of March 10, it was my turn to get on the bus that took us to the Vienna airport. We loaded this huge four-engined plane that had United States Air Force painted on it. I had never been on an airplane before, never even seen one except for the ones that spread propaganda from the air. The planes that bombed us during the war were never seen by us children, for we were in the shelter during the air raids. The sound they produced however will always stay in my memory.

I got a window seat and a young lady of about my age sat next to me. I remember her face with lots of makeup and bright red lipstick on her lips. To me the whole sight was ugly, and on top of that, the poor thing threw up numerous times during the flight. Did I care? Heck no! I was on my way to the United States of America!

The plane took off in late afternoon from Vienna, and stopped for fuel in Dublin, Ireland. Late that night the plane took off again. We traveled at night, and most of us slept or tried to sleep, while the unfortunate girl next to me was emptying herself into the barf bag. We landed at the air force base in Newfoundland, Canada, at 3:00 A.M. We were asked to leave the plane for a short stopover, and were warned to dress warmly because of the outside temperature. Sure enough, when they opened the door, the air hit all of us. As we were walking down the ramp and into the building, the cold air got through to our bones. I was used to cold weather in Hungary, but this coldness I had never experienced before. Inside

No Regrets

the building they gave us some food, but many didn't touch it, as they were airsick. Luckily, I had no trouble eating.

About 6:00 A.M. the plane took off again. Daylight was slowly creeping in the cabin. I looked outside but the only thing I saw was snow everywhere. As the day got brighter, I realized that we were flying above the clouds. Nothing but blue skies and white cloud tops all around us. In the early afternoon the plane landed again, but this time in the United States at McGuire Air Force Base in New Jersey. There were loud cheers coming from many parts of the plane; people were elated with joy. I was also part of the jubilation.

We exited the plane one by one, walking down the steps of the ramp. When I stepped on the ground, I dropped on my knees and kissed it. I didn't care what people around me thought. I was glad to be in the country which I knew would open its door to me, take me in, and adopt me, giving me a chance for a new life. I didn't have a penny in my pocket. What I had were survival skills and a good work ethic. That is worth a lot more than money.

The date was March 11, 1957. I was nineteen years old.

8

Life in America

My life in the United States—the beginning years

Before coming to this country this is how I pictured the U.S. after listening to people while in Europe: the streets are paved with gold; money grows on trees; every family owns a home, and each home has a double garage with two cars in it. The only part of the myth I believed was ownership of a home and cars. These people forgot to mention the most important thing that was offered by the U.S., namely: freedom. Material things were placed in higher importance than freedom. Little did they know, and little did I know. It didn't take me long to find out that the U.S. was offering something most other countries did not. This great country is a land of many opportunities. I have never worked so hard in my life as in the U.S., but with hard work I was able to move forward and make a life for myself. The possibilities are endless for someone who is willing to work hard.

We were directed to a bunch of blue-colored buses with U.S. Air Force painted on the sides. As soon as we were aboard, the buses hit the main highway. This road was a different kind than we had in Hungary or even in Austria at that time. These were

No Regrets

wide roads with many lanes and lots of cars traveling them. It was dark but I had no trouble seeing the signs: New York City this way, Boston that way, etc. I was soaking up the scenery. I found out later that we were in New Jersey, traveling towards Camp Kilmer, an army base that was reopened strictly for the Hungarian refugees as a place to register and a temporary holding place. At the camp we were issued bedding, toilet articles, eating utensils, and a very important booklet: a Hungarian-English dictionary. This was a lifesaver for years to come.

American soldiers who had a crash course in the Hungarian language directed us. They tried to speak to us but it was almost impossible to understand. I remember one word very clearly that was said to us by one of the soldiers: "everybody." I had no idea what "everybody" meant, and neither did anybody else except one guy who thought he knew English. This Hungarian ding-dong tried to impress all of us, and was yelling at the top of his lungs that the soldier wants us to go that way and not this way, etc. As I look back it had nothing to do with the word "everybody." I had met the first "túl okos" (know-it-all) person in the new world.

My stay at Camp Kilmer was short. The HIAS organization sent me to Washington, D.C., because Zoli was already there. The apartment was in Alexandria, Virginia, across the Potomac River from D.C. I remember it being small, but cheery and bright. There were many yellow colors in the room. Actually, as I recall, Zoli had already gone to New York City, the place he always wanted to be.

By the next day, I had a job lined up as an automobile mechanic at a Chrysler-Plymouth dealership, and at the same time I received my social security card. I'm very proud of the fact that I have been putting into the system since my very first paying job in the U.S.

Somebody from the dealership picked me up in the mornings, driving across the river into Washington, D.C., and turning left at the first traffic circle to get to the shop. I was working

Life in America

on brakes and other simple jobs like minor tune-ups. I thought I was doing good work and was having a good time doing it. I was to be paid minimum wage, which at that time was $1.00.

Friday was payday and I was to receive my very first pay in the United States. I had worked forty hours that week and I was to receive close to $40.00, minus some money taken out for taxes. I figured wrong. My paycheck was showing $20.00 and I almost went to the roof. Welcome to the United States, László Veres! What an eye opener! With the dictionary in my hands, I went to see the owner to question the small size of my paycheck. With the help from my dictionary, I translated what he was told me: "You don't speak English yet." I fumbled through the dictionary and in some way I was able to tell him what a son-of-a-bitch he was and gave him the international "up-yours" sign that needed no translation. By early Monday morning I was at the Union Station in Washington, D.C.

I knew that Detroit was the place to be for an automobile mechanic to find work. I wanted to go to Detroit, but didn't have enough money. I did have enough for a ticket to Cleveland. I took the train and I was on to new adventures. What was waiting for me there?

In Cleveland the train station is located next to the factory district. I started to walk down Payne Street (I think that is the name) and walked into the very first factory. It was a larger shop that produced different types of lamps. The foreman hired me on the spot and put me to work. He showed me what to do and I did it. He was satisfied and left me alone. My job was to polish the brassy part of the lamp on a machine. I went at it with full gusto. The foreman came by many times telling me "take it easy." He hired me at $1.15 an hour, a nice increase in pay from my first job. I must have done good work because in a week I received a raise to $1.25, and a few weeks later, another to $1.45. Except for the money that was taken out for taxes, they paid me in full as they promised.

Sometime in May I received information that the rest of

my family arrived and were at a hotel in New York City. I told my foreman that I had to go to see my parents and that I would be back. He understood. I went to the Greyhound station, bought a ticket, and I was on my way.

Of course it was good to see everybody together again. I wanted to see the tallest skyscraper in the world, the Empire State Building. I walked to it and took the express elevator to the ninety-sixth floor, then transferred to another one that took us to the observation deck where one could walk around and see forever. It was an incredible sight, especially in the evening, when all the city lights were turned on. It was also scary up there. The constantly blowing wind puts the building into a swaying motion. It was still fun. Coming down wasn't much fun. The express elevator's descent is so fast that feels like one's stomach will hit the ceiling. It felt good to walk on the pavement again.

Next day we sat down with the HIAS representative and were given opportunities to go to one of the three cities where they would sponsor us: Dallas, Milwaukee, and Boston. My parents looked at me and asked the question: "Laci (that's me), what do you think?" I replied that I had never heard of either Dallas or Milwaukee, however, I did hear about Boston because of the famous schools there. It was decided that the Veres family would settle in Boston. I still send a $100.00 check to the HIAS every year, so that organization may continue their services to other immigrants.

I had to get back to Cleveland to get my few things together. I had to take care of some business like paying my landlord for the rent I owed, and say good-bye to the workers at the lamp factory. They passed the hat among themselves, and as a going away present they gave me the collected cash. I thanked them many times for their generosity. I guess I had made an impression on them. By afternoon I was on the Greyhound again. In New York we boarded the train and the Veres family was on their way to Boston.

Life in America

Life in Boston

We moved into an apartment on Nightingale Street in Dorchester, a suburb of Boston. The neighbors were lovely people who came to offer their help as soon as we arrived. They brought material things like a piece of carpet or a piece of furniture to make our apartment more friendly. My father assigned names to these people and my parents referred to them as the "Carpet Lady," or the Furniture Man," etc., depending what they gave us. Until we purchased a TV for ourselves, we were invited by one of our neighbors to watch the tube at their home. My parents had a name for them also: "Mr. and Mrs. Television."

Because of my trade, I was the first one to get a job.

I was hired at a Buick dealership and worked in the repair shop. They were very pleased with me and after work I told my parents how satisfied they were with my performance and work habit. About two weeks later I was laid off and I went home crying, totally disappointed. The problem was the lack of knowledge of the English language, although the excuse they told me was that the dealership had to make room for union workers. I cried like a little baby on my mother's shoulders, and like a typical Jewish loving mother she comforted me. She made me feel better by telling me that there would be many other opportunities for me. "There will be many hurdles along the way and this was just one of them," she told me.

In a few days I had a job working at a De Soto car dealership as a mechanic (they don't make De Soto cars anymore). Again, I was let go about a week later with the same reason: I couldn't speak English. This time I didn't cry and wasn't even disappointed. I went on looking for other opportunities.

In a day or so, I was hired by a Nash-Rambler dealership as a mechanic. I had my longest tenure at that place and I could have stayed there, but this time I was the one who decided to move on when I received an offer from New York City.

During this time I wanted to get a driver's license and I put a major effort into studying for it. This was in June and I had been in this country for less than three months. My English was getting better as I was adding more and more words to my vocabulary each day. For one to receive a driver's license it required much more knowledge. To receive a driver's license in the state of Massachusetts at that time, one had to pass an oral exam in the English language. Not an easy task for someone who was new to this country.

László still does minor work on his car.

I went to a driver's school and picked up a driver's manual, and attended some classes. I knew how to drive, that was not the problem; the problem was with the speaking part. A young lady at that school offered her help in my quest. She was about my age, possibly couple of years younger. She must have liked me for she was very patient with me as I slowly made some progress. I went

Friends of the Tucson Pops Orchestra

P.O. Box 14545, Tucson, AZ 85732-4545 • (520) 722-5853

RECEIPT

Date: 5/28/06

Name: Crosby Leslie

Address: 9850 E Calle Puchu

City/State/Zip:

Received by: DS

	Qty.	Membership	T-Shirt	
		$50.00	$Ø	
			$65.00	
			$65.00	

Thank you!

This contribution is tax deductable.

home and started to memorize a question first, followed by the answer that went with the question from the manual. In most cases I had no idea of what I was talking about. I just kept on memorizing, and when I heard a question I knew what answer went with it.

Next time I saw her, she decided to test me. She couldn't believe what she was hearing. She couldn't believe that someone could learn so much English in a week's time. Little did she know, that I just memorized the whole manual without understanding most of the material in it. She was more than pleased and told me that I was ready to take the driver's test at the Motor Vehicle Division.

The test was twofold: oral exam first, followed with a driver's test. After answering many questions, to my big surprise the examiner told me to go outside for the driving portion of the exam. I passed the oral and I was almost screaming with joy. One of the workers from the dealership accompanied me for this test, and let me use his car. About an hour later I was a proud owner of a driver's license. I went back to see that young lady again to thank her for all her help. I never saw her again after that.

Life in New York City

Zoli was in New York City during this time, working, but I'm not sure where. One day I received a phone call from him telling me that the soccer team in New York expressed an interest in me, and as a payoff, they would get a job for me that paid $5.00 per hour. That was a huge increase from what I was making as a mechanic. I was interested in the money, plus I wanted to play soccer again. I talked over this offer with my parents and they agreed that I should try my luck in New York. I was to stay with my aunt and uncle and pay rent to them for the use of one of their rooms. They lived in Union City, New Jersey, close to the Lincoln Tunnel that connected to New York.

As promised, the soccer team got me a job as a carpenter

in a furniture factory. What did I know about carpentry? Absolutely nothing. The pay was $5.00 an hour and the work was easy. I was attending soccer practice for the New York Italian team that was made up of a bunch of foreigners like me, but mainly Italians. I took the bus across the Lincoln Tunnel, changed to a subway, and that is how I got to my work place.

New York City is like no other place. There is much to see and much to do. The streets are always busy and noisy. It seemed like the city never slept.

Everything was going well until the union started to complain that their members could not get a job, because us non-union people were filling the empty places. The factory buckled under the union's demand and I was without a job again. I told the soccer team good-bye and I was on my way back to Boston. My stay in New York City lasted for only about two months but it wasn't a waste of time; it was a good learning experience.

While I was gone, my parents moved to another apartment building on Blue Hill Avenue. This place was a step up, although wasn't far from the other place. We were on the third floor, which was the top of the building. Being on the top has advantages and disadvantages. It is nice and warm during the winter because the lower floors heat the top; on the other hand, summers are very hot, as we were so close to the roof.

Back in Boston again and the Hungarian Club

As a welcome home present my parents bought me a car. It was a 1951 Chevy, a beautiful, shiny, black color. I thought it was the most beautiful thing on wheels. I remember my father paying $400.00 for it. My responsibility was to pay for the insurance and gas. The car was in good condition and ran nicely. I loved that car.

I managed to get a job in a shoe factory, working for Embo Casual Footwear Company. It produced low-cost shoes, most of them being exported to South American countries. At this place

Life in America

the knowledge of the English language wasn't of major importance. Most of the workers around me were from Italy and I felt like I was in Italy from hearing all the Italian language spoken. My foreman's name was Benny Katz, born in Czechoslovakia. He was a Holocaust survivor. He spoke about five languages, including Hungarian. He was practicing his Hungarian on me, while I desperately wanted to learn English. He was good to me.

I was put on a machine that burned designs into the soles before they were glued to the shoe with a press. I was asked if I wanted to be paid by the hourly wage or by piecework. Piecework meant that I would be paid according to the amount of work I was producing. There was no question that I wanted piecework. I knew my working habits; hard work never scared me. I was taking home good-sized paychecks and I was also getting careless with my money.

My parents decided to talk to me about it and a decision was made: I was to turn over some money to them for rent, food, and laundry. The rest of the money I could keep for spending. Little did I know, my father was putting my money into the bank week after week, creating a savings account for me.

There was a Hungarian club in Boston and I start attending it. The club was a nice place to be. Most of the people were from the same part of Budapest as we were from. I made a good friend who was about a year older than I. He was a regular visitor at our home and my parents liked him a lot. His name was Ervin. He had no car at the time and rode with me to many places.

At the club I found out that Hungarians were forming a soccer club and I wanted to be part of it. At the same time I was already playing on the Boston-Italian team. I didn't like their style of soccer; they were more interested in kicking bodies than the ball. I remember at one of the games I kicked the winning goal in the final seconds against their big rival team. All the spectators rushed on the field in their jubilation and carried me off as their hero. I never played for that team again.

No Regrets

The newly formed Hungarian/American team started to play against different teams of other nationalities. On one occasion during the game I got a major charley horse in my calf muscles. I was very much in pain and my teammates had to carry me off the field. I was lying on my back with closed eyes, shaking my calf muscles, trying to ease the pain. I felt someone touching my leg, asking me if I would mind having it rubbed. I opened my eyes and a very pretty girl was smiling at me. She started to massage my legs and I enjoyed it tremendously. I wasn't in a hurry to re-enter the game even though I felt better. Some of my teammates were making comments like, "My legs need to be massaged too, Magda." That is how I found out her name. I told her my name was Laci, she replied, "I know." After the game we walked to the car together and rode back to the Hungarian club with some others. Magda's friend was with us also; her name was Ina, a girl from Italy. They were the closest of friends.

Magda and I started to date and became very close. She was two years younger than I, and she lived in Somerville with her aunt and uncle, who came to this country in the 1930s. The aunt's name was Helen and she was very pleasant to be around, while her husband was just the opposite. One day I introduced Magda to my parents. My father didn't approve of her; he didn't approve of any girl we boys brought to the house. I continued seeing her anyway.

Before I met Magda, I had an eye for another young lady at the Hungarian club. She was just about my age, but with a lot more experience in romantic affairs. Her name was Gizi. After a dance we sat down and she offered a cigarette to me. I told her I didn't smoke. She kept pushing. Finally, she told me that I was a chicken and started to walk away from me. I should have let her go, but me being dumb and stupid, I stopped her and told her to give me a cigarette. I was about to show her I wasn't a chicken. That was probably the most unintelligent and dumbest decision I ever made in my life. I smoked for about nine years before I quit "cold turkey," one of the smartest things I ever did. My relationship

Life in America

with Gizi ended very shortly; actually there was no relationship at all. She wasn't for me at all, but Magda was at the time.

Moving ahead

I decided that it was time to break away from the Hungarian club and the constant talking in Hungarian. It was time for me to learn the language of my adopted country. I signed up for night school where English language was offered for foreigners. It was fun to hear the different accents in the class. There were Italians, Poles, Germans, some Orientals, and one Hungarian, me. The class was from 7:00-9:00 P.M. on Tuesdays and Thursdays. In the class we were forced to speak English, and the lady teacher refused to let anybody talk among themselves in their native tongue. Magda was attending high school in Cambridge and she is the one who told me about the night classes that were offered at her school.

One of those nights after class I was introduced to a gentleman who greeted me in Hungarian. He was not a member of the class but was from the International Institute of Boston, as I found out. He was a middle-aged man, well-dressed and well-mannered, and had a very pleasant speaking voice. In his flawless Hungarian asked me about what was on my mind for the future, and wanted to know what I did back in the old country. Among other things, I mentioned to him my musical experience at the Béla Bartók Music Conservatory. He said that he would get in touch with Budapest, and get proof of my membership there. I told him not to bother because I had the certificate from the conservatory in my possession at home. He asked me to bring it next time.

Before my parents left Budapest, they put together some very important papers and some photos and carried those with them. Among the papers they carried were my birth certificate and the certificate from the conservatory. My parents were very sharp people, thinking way ahead into the future. I took my certificate to this man. He sat down at his typewriter and page-by-page translated the document into English. When he was finished he told me that the translation had to be notarized by the Commonwealth of Massachusetts to make it legal. He also told me that he would get in touch with me in a few days.

As promised, the call came in a few days and an appointment was made with the Admissions Office of the New England Conservatory of Music on Huntington Avenue, across from Boston Symphony Hall. We turned in the papers and within a few days I was notified that I was accepted into one of the world's most prestigious music schools. I didn't have to audition for the New England Conservatory; the Music Academy in Budapest that was named after one of the greatest composers of twentieth century must have had status. It must have carried a great worldwide reputation for it was good enough for the conservatory.

Boston, age 19

A dance gig in Boston, 1958

In the fall of 1958 I started to take clarinet lessons under the guidance of Felix Viscuglia, a member of the Boston Symphony. I was paying for my tuition; after all, I had a good paying job.

Life in America

When my close friend Ervin found out that I was attending night school and was just accepted into the conservatory, his visits to our home became fewer and fewer, and the communication between the two of us slowly faded away. My guess is that he didn't like the fact that I was making something out of myself.

On my teacher's recommendation I was accepted into two orchestras: first into the Quincy Symphony where I played second clarinet, but moved up to principal the following season; and into the Cambridge Symphony as second clarinetist. My teacher's reputation and influence carried a heavy weight, because I was accepted into the Cambridge orchestra which performed at a very high level. Some of its members were regular subs in the Boston Pops. Magda liked what I was doing and so did my parents. I was moving on.

At home Jancsi and Gyuri were attending middle school and they were learning English at a very fast pace. Pista was working someplace as a dishwasher first; later on I took him in to the shoe factory. When he was old enough he asked me to teach him how to drive, which I did. He was a fast learner.

If I recall correctly, eventually Gyuri also ended up at the shoe place. I understand that after I left for the army the factory burned down and was never rebuilt again in the same location.

Father was working as a laborer in a warehouse and my mother was slowly making connections to do some sewing. She was a seamstress in the old country, and a very fine one at that. One day my father came home from work and told us that he quit his job. We were disappointed, but he wasn't.

He decided that he would become a house painter and paperhanger. Our next-door neighbor was his first customer. This was nothing but trial and error on his part and we boys helped him as much as we could. Paper hanging is a specialty-type job; one really has to have the know-how that is required. He was frustrated; papers had to be taken off many times, put back up again only to turn out crooked, or the lines wouldn't line up, etc. Our father is one of the most hardheaded people I have ever known. He stayed with the job, learned as he went along, and although the job took forever to finish, he finished it. The neighbor felt sorry for him for spending so much time on it, and offered extra money to my father. He promptly refused it. He accepted only the money that was negotiated for and not a penny more. He knew he lost his shirt on that job, but he didn't care.

Through this neighbor of ours, jobs were slowly coming in and with each job he got better and better. In a few years he became one of the most respected painters in the Boston area. Future customers were willing to wait up to a year for Béla Veres to work on their home. In the early sixties he started to work on outside painting jobs also. However, for the two story homes he needed to build scaffolds. For that he needed to be licensed and had to have a special permit for the job. To be able to get a license he had to pass a written test, yet his command of the English language was non-existent for an examination like that.

Years later, while I was back in Boston on leave from the army, my father asked me to go with him to the county building as an interpreter to get his license. We talked to a gentleman in charge who was very polite and explained that it was Mr. Veres who had to take a test without me being there as a translator. As I was translating, the conversation was going back and forth between the two of them with me being in the middle. My father insisted that I keep telling the man that he was a well-trained professional painter in the old country with almost forty years of experience and that should qualify him for the permit. Finally, father gave in and we went home, but two days later we were back. The same conversation took place and father kept telling me to tell him about his tremendous experience from the old country. Father had a tendency to color his speech with some fancy Hungarian cussing words and at times I cracked up laughing. I had a difficult time keeping a straight face while I was translating, carefully blipping out the words that no dictionary contained. We were sent home

Life in America

again, but were back again, slowly becoming a regular fixture on the second floor of the county seat building. My father wasn't about to give up!

I had to leave Boston when my leave from the army expired. Later I found out that his consistent perseverance paid off, and in the end the person in charge granted him the permit and made a comment that in all his years of working there he had never met a more determined man than our father. That was our father! Jancsi, the youngest of my brothers, joined the business eventually, and with hard work the two of them created a lucrative business for themselves.

No Regrets

*A proud member of the
United States Army, 1960*

9

The U.S. Army

United States Army

Before I came to the United States, I was well aware of the fact that I had to register for the Selective Service System within three months of my arrival, meaning that I could be drafted into the military. To me this was no big deal; it was a small price to pay for the privilege of coming to the U.S.

One day after work my mother handed me an envelope addressed to me. She was looking over my shoulder as I was reading it; she wanted to see what that official-looking envelope was all about. It was a conscription notice; I was drafted into the United States Army and ordered to report on August 30, 1960, at Fort Dix, New Jersey. First I had to have a physical exam given by army doctors. A bunch of us new recruits were lined up like an assembly line, totally naked, and had to perform the "bend down and cough" routine, while the doctors grabbed some of our private parts. What a job, I thought to myself.

I received my draft papers in late June, giving me ample time to say good-bye to members of the orchestras I played in and to my colleagues at the shoe factory. I went to the Fourth of July

No Regrets

Esplanade Concert featuring the Boston Pops Orchestra, with Arthur Fiedler conducting. My teacher from the conservatory was playing in the orchestra that evening and I had a chance to talk to him backstage during intermission. I told him about the draft and he wished me good luck. He also said something that I shall never forget: "Wherever you go, you will be well known." What did he see in me, I asked myself. We hugged each other, then left as intermission was almost over. The annual Fourth of July concert is still presented by the Boston Pops (now called the Esplanade Orchestra) free to the public. The concert is attended by tens of thousands of people and is held on Boston's side of the Charles River, which separates Boston from Cambridge.

It was difficult to say good-bye to Magda. We had grown very close to each other and were even talking about marriage after the service. Her letters were always comforting and eagerly awaited during basic training. We exchanged letters while I was in Arizona, but again the correspondence slowly faded away. Most likely it was my fault.

The day I left my parents' home was a sad day for them. I had to report to the recruit station at the navy yard and from there a bus would take us to Fort Dix, where we would stay until they shipped us out to basic training. Pista, who became the new owner of the Chevy, drove Father and me to the subway station. Father and I got out of the car. I was going to the downtown direction while he was heading the opposite way. We hugged and I saw the same teary eyes as in Budapest. He kissed me many times and I kissed his face, tasting his tears. I was on my way, not knowing that for me Boston would be just a place to visit in the future. I have to admit that I loved Boston. The city had a European feel. I have many fond memories of that city.

At Fort Dix we were given our GI supplies that stayed with us until discharge. At that place we received our first famous GI haircuts. I have never seen so many young men cry as they were coming out of the barber's shop. Smiling faces were nowhere to

The U.S. Army

be seen and neither were there any bald heads, for everybody covered their heads with their assigned GI hat. After the last person was finished with his buzz, we had to get in a group for a group photo. While most of the recruits were crying over their lost locks, having a picture taken was like putting salt on an open wound. The amazing thing is that the picture came out with everybody smiling. Just before the photographer shot the picture he told us to say "pussy." That did the trick.

At Fort Dix the army gave us different types of tests to find out where the military could make best use of us. After evaluating the tests, the military's decision was that I would be assigned to the Signal Corps after basic training. This was upsetting for me. When I received my draft papers, immediately I went to the Selective Service and asked how could I get into the Army Band. I was told that signing up for an extra year would guarantee my request. To me it was worth it to be in the discipline where I wanted to be, even though it meant an extra year.

Basic training

I took my basic training at Fort Benning, Georgia. I heard things about basic training in any army; I knew there would be lots of harassment, but I also knew that it would be over in eight weeks. The lieutenant in charge of our platoon made me a squad leader on the drill sergeant's recommendation. During the sixth week of the camp I was called in to the captain's office. After I did my salute and said in a loud voice, "Recruit László Veres reporting, sir," he told me to "at ease." In so many words he told me that I was a fine soldier, and recommendation was made that I should attend officer's school after basic training. I told him that I would have to think about it. The following weekend I called home and asked my father's opinion on this matter. He told me that it was totally up to me, but added, "Being in the U.S. military as an officer is a great honor and could provide a fine career." I thought about it and made my choice. When the captain called me in again about my decision, I told him that while I appreciated his suggestion, my preference was to be a civilian after my discharge three years from then. There was disappointment on his face but he didn't hold a grudge against me for the remaining two weeks of training.

An American soldier at basic training, Ft. Benning, Ga.

Spit-shining the army boots, Ft. Benning, Ga., 1960.

The U.S. Army

One day a fellow soldier was interested in finding out where I was from since I "talked funny," as he put it. I replied that I was from Boston. He looked at me, puzzled, and after a long silence he spoke, "You know, my grandmother always told me that people in Boston do talk funny." I didn't respond to his statement.

After basic training we were transferred to Fort Gordon, Georgia, to the Signal School. I pulled my share of K.P. (kitchen police) for a whole week before the training classes started. It was an eight-week course, and I totally disliked it. I wanted to be assigned to the band. I complained a lot, to no avail. I was told that at my next assigned location I should talk to the commanding officer in charge.

After the session was over we were given a ten-day leave. I took the train to Boston. Magda knew my arrival time; she was waiting for me. It was good to see her. I didn't bother to let my parents know of my arrival time; it was 10:30 A.M. and I knew they would be at work. That afternoon I went home and everybody was glad to see me. My parents were extremely proud to see me in my uniform. My furlough days went by very fast; before I realized it, I had report back to Fort Gordon. This time my parents accompanied me to the train station. I had said my good-bye to Magda the night before, not knowing that fourteen years would pass before I would see her again, and then only for a short visit.

Fort Huachuca, Arizona

I didn't find out where I was to be transferred until I got back to Fort Gordon. My new assignment was for Fort Huachuca, Arizona. I had never heard of the state of Arizona, never mind Fort Huachuca.

We got on the train and were on our way. Soldiers were talking about snakes and scorpions and lizards that lived in the Arizona desert. They were also talking about Indians, how they scalped people. I must say I cried a lot. I was from the big cities:

Budapest, Vienna, Boston, New York; what was I to do in the desert in the middle of nowhere? Slowly I settled down and decided that everything would work out just fine, and in the end it did.

As soon as I arrived at the base I asked for permission to see the officer in charge of the band. I did tell him that the reason I added an extra year to my military duty was to be in the band. He asked me to play. His name was Warrant Officer Gramish. He invited First Sergeant Johnson to sit in on the audition. Although I was totally out of shape, I managed to play excerpts from my solo repertoire. A few days later I received my new assignment as Bandsman. I became a member of the 36th U.S. Army Band. This took place in the middle of January 1961.

The base was located right next to Sierra Vista, a small town in the early 1960s. Mainly army personnel and civilians working on base lived there. It did have a high school but not much else. Today it is one of the fastest growing cities in Arizona and becoming one of the largest, excluding Phoenix and Tucson.

Life in the 36th Army Band

In the barracks there were about twenty bunks lined up next to each other. Most of the career bandsmen lived off base with their families. Being in the band was an easy life, perfect for me for I had plenty of free time, which I devoted to practicing my clarinet. Yes, we had to wake up at a certain hour; beds had to be made; individual cubicles had to be kept clean. There were showers, sinks, and a row of toilets, about six of them next to each other, without any privacy. All these were located in one place. I adapted to the conditions very easily. The mess hall was only a short distance away. The food was fine; luckily I'm not a fussy eater.

Our daily routine included rehearsal in the mornings and playing "retreat" every day except Sundays in front of the base headquarters, where the flagpole was located. The rest of the hours were free. For entertainment there was a pool table in the recreation

The U.S. Army

room with T.V. I decided to use my free time for practicing, putting in about two hours a day. One day a new soldier was transferred to the band. His name was Gray Rains. Having him join the thirty-two-piece Army Band was a blessing, for he turned out to be an inspiration for me.

The very first day Gray showed up, without talking to anybody he went into one of the rooms and started to play his trumpet. The beautiful trumpet tone he was producing got my attention. At first the only thing he did was to play a sequence of long notes that lasted for about twenty to thirty minutes. Then came scales and other basic exercises. An hour went by and he was still playing. Then another hour followed another one. Other bandsmen started to talk to each other: "Who is this guy, and what is he trying to do?" Five hours later he stopped practicing, packed up his instrument, and left the barracks. Since he was married he lived off base. This was on a Sunday, when most people just hung around taking it easy. I was impressed. Listening to Gray showed me what true discipline is required to master an instrument. His practice schedule was structured, every detail worked out to its finest points.

Gray did this day after day; to him time was never to be wasted. One day I approached him and asked, "What are your goals with your instrument?" and he replied, "I want to join the Stan Kenton Band after discharge." In those years the Stan Kenton Band was one of the greatest jazz bands in the world. After that conversation I felt inspired to practice my instrument more than ever. I was always motivated, but this time I felt truly enthused about my playing. My daily practice schedule went from two hours a day to five or six. "If he can do it, I can do it also," became my motto. I knew I overdid the practicing, for one of my front teeth got so loose that it had to be pulled a year later, replaced by a false one. My embouchure (lips formation) had to go through a major change to be able to play again. While in the army Gray and I became good colleagues.

A side comment about Gray: after I got transferred to

No Regrets

Germany we lost touch. About eight years went by when I received a phone call from Gray. He asked me if I remembered him. I told him of course, and asked how he was doing and what he was doing. His reply didn't surprise me at all: "I've been touring with the Kenton band." I told him congratulations and how proud I was of him. Before we hung up he thanked me for being an inspiration in his life. I was shocked! "What did I do?" I asked myself, as Gray was the one who motivated me to become a better player. He told me that by listening to my beautiful tone and musical phrasing, he himself turned out to be a better musician. Without realizing it, we were pushing each other to better ourselves. Gray had a vision and with his hard work ethic he accomplished his aspirations; proving that total dedication to a cause will produce results. I never heard from him again. Forty years have gone by since the last time I saw him. Because of his work ethic I truly believe that he had a successful musical career. I hope he is doing well.

In the band I was asked if I played saxophone, and I told them yes. I wasn't very fond of that instrument but played it fairly well. I loved my clarinet. I joined the 36th Army Band's Dance Band by playing second alto. Playing in the dance band was a great experience for me in more ways than one. There were some fine "jazz-ers" around me; Gray being one of them, also First Sergeant Johnson on lead alto. Besides learning another side of music (I always cared only for classical music), my horizon opened up. Playing in the dance band also introduced me to some very important people in the military. We played lots of dance jobs in the officers' club, and during the breaks I had a chance to talk to some high-ranking officers. We were not allowed to approach them; some of them came to talk to us.

One colonel was very interested in my background and asked many questions. Colonel Fisher was a very gentle human being and very friendly. He had children, but they were all grown, and had families of their own He invited me to his house to have dinner with him and his wife. He also asked me if I would be

The U.S. Army

willing to talk about my life in front of people. I told him I would. One early Sunday morning we drove to Tucson to a church on East 22nd Street to talk to the congregation. My English was on very shaky ground but the people in attendance appreciated my stories and gave me a big ovation. I was invited to the Fisher home many times, where I enjoyed Mrs. Fisher's fine cooking.

The 36th Army Dance Band at Ft. Huachuca. Gray Rains second from left in back row; Sgt. Brown on bass; and Sgt. Johnson in middle of saxophone section. László is to his right.

As soon as I arrived at Fort Huachuca and settled in the band, I wanted to take clarinet lessons again. After some detective work I contacted the Tucson Symphony's principal clarinet player, James Glasgow, on the phone. I introduced myself and told him about my interest in taking some lessons from him. He asked me about my background. After I mentioned to him the places I studied, he told me that he didn't have any openings. However, he recommended a Dr. Fain, professor of clarinet at the University of Arizona, as a possible teacher. I was always interested in studying, and in due course I studied with some of the world's renowned teachers including some tutoring with Mitchell Lurie, and many chats with Keith Stein who thought highly of my playing.

In 1974 I spent a summer at Tanglewood, where I

continued my studies with Felix Viscuglia, member of the Boston Symphony, and attended master classes given by Harold Wright, principal clarinetist of the same orchestra. The following summer I was in Aspen attending master classes given by Leon Russianoff, eventually taking lessons from him. Leon was one of the greatest teachers of the clarinet; his students held principal clarinet positions in many of the orchestras, including overseas.

At one of Russianoff's master classes he asked for volunteers to perform at the next session. I expressed interest to perform in front of the class because I wanted to hear the great teacher's evaluation of my playing. The next day graduate students from Julliard and the Manhattan School of Music (both prestigious institutions) were performing one by one. Clarinet players were scared and soon found out why. To perform in front of a bunch of clarinet players was scary enough, but that was nothing compared to Russianoff's criticism; which at times was horrifying. Nevertheless, at the same time one could learn a great deal from the man. He had the gift to take students apart despite his diplomatic approach. As the players performed, every one of them were stopped after playing just a few notes. None of the players had a chance to play more than half a line of the music and they were all fine clarinetists. It was my turn to play.

The musical selection to be played was Stravinsky's "Three Pieces for Clarinet Alone." I chose the second movement. I started to play, anticipating being stopped right away just like the players ahead of me. There was silence from Russianoff. I went on and finished the first line. Still silence; no thunderous "stop!" or "no!" coming from him. I kept going, gaining more and more confidence. I felt good and I was getting immersed in the music. Finally it was over. Dead silence was hovering around the whole area. I was afraid to look up when suddenly I heard one person applauding. I looked up and to my big surprise it was Russianoff. The rest of the musicians started to give a round of applause also and as soon as everyone quieted down he spoke for the first time, "You are a great artist." He took me as a student during my stay in Aspen.

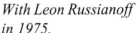
With Leon Russianoff in 1975.

One day I went to the university and introduced myself to Dr. Fain. He was a very nice gentleman but refused to take me as a student, using his poor health as the reason. He told me to see a Dr. Jones, one of the new young professors in the woodwind department. Dr. Jones' office was across the hallway. Disappointed and discouraged, I walked over to Dr. Jones' office, but his door was closed as he was giving a bassoon lesson to a student. While standing outside waiting, a middle-age man standing at the door started to talk to me. Our conversation led to Boston and eventually to the New England Conservatory. He got very excited when he heard the conservatory being mentioned and he asked who my teacher was. When I told him it was Felix Viscuglia, he almost went through the roof. By this time, other students wanting to hear the conversation surrounded us. He told me that he knew Viscuglia very well; he studied with him and they were good friends. When Dr. Jones' office finally opened, he ran into the studio and with an excited voice he said, "Wendall, you've got to meet this man and hear him play his clarinet; he studied with Viscuglia and would like to take lessons from you." Dr. Wendall Jones, a young-looking, tall man with a warm smile, showed himself at the door with an outstretched hand for a handshake and invited me into his studio. After hearing me play he told me that he would take me as a student.

No Regrets

This was the beginning of a long-lasting friendship. I would travel to Tucson every other weekend to take my lessons, which proved to be valuable in many ways.

When I arrived at Fort Huachuca my rank was "private," one step above "recruit." In a few months I became "Pfc" (private first class) and about six months later "Sp4" (specialist 4). Each time I moved up in rank the monthly pay increased accordingly. To move up to a higher rank than Sp4, one had to become a career soldier. We were given a chance to qualify for "pro-pay." Requirements were the knowledge of all major/minor scales, corresponding arpeggios by memory throughout the instrument, plus other stuff. I qualified and augmented my paycheck by $13.00 per month. Back in 1961 it was a good-size increase; especially when comparing to today's prices. A gallon of gasoline was nineteen cents and the minimum wage $1.00 or $1.25.

There were many interesting people in the band who came from different places with diverse backgrounds. Some were constant complainers and I tried to stay away from them. I wasn't interested in listening to the non-stop moaning and griping of most of the players. Their musical background consisted of nothing more than playing their instruments in their respective high school bands, while among the enlisted career soldiers, some were reasonably good performers. One exception was First Sergeant Johnson who was an outstanding clarinet/saxophone player. Besides being a terrific musician he was also a wonderful human being. I was puzzled as to why he choose military life with his great talent, until I found out that he had a large family of nine children and couldn't afford to leave the military. The 36th Army Band was lucky to have him.

The person who shared the cubicle next to me was a black person who played the clarinet. I never knew his real name; everybody called him "Slow Motion." The title fit him well, for besides being slow in moving, he also walked like a duck. Arriving back at the barracks from dinner, either the record player or the

The U.S. Army

radio was always on. One evening the music being aired from the radio was from some ballet. Although I wasn't familiar with the composition, it was beautiful. All of a sudden Mr. Slow Motion jumped out of his bed and picked up a broom. The broom became his dancing partner and with the greatest of grace, elegance, and ease, he was gliding across the barracks in beautiful motion. Everyone around was spellbound, and I was no exception. When he finished, he returned the broom to the closet and in his slow motion way walked back to his bed. I told him that his performance was dazzling and after thanking me he told me that he was a dancer before being drafted into the service.

The next night I invited him to go to town with me and said, "I'll buy you a beer." There was a bowling alley outside the army post with a bar in it and we headed in that direction. Slow Motion stopped me and his comment shocked me: "They don't allow black people in there." I experienced segregation against black people for the first time. Being raised in a different country, in my naïve way, I always thought that only Jews experienced discrimination. I told him, "The hell with them; let's go across the street to the Mexican restaurant and have a cold beer there." We had a great visit.

One day I woke up in the early morning with an incredible stomach pain and took myself to sick call. The doctor sent me back to the barracks telling me that I was faking the pain to get out of some military duty. In the barrack I laid down but the pain was excruciating and in a few hours I had to be carried back to the hospital. This time they did a short examination on me and took a blood test. As soon as the result came back I was rushed to the operating table for my appendix had to be removed. I was lucky. It was taken out just before it ruptured. My parents were worried sick and took the Greyhound across the country to visit me. They spent over two days on the bus to see their child. My parents were something else. Their love for their children cannot be calculated.

Many band members came to visit me, one of them being a

horn player by the name of Fred Murch. In those days smoking was allowed in hospitals and that's what he was doing during the visit. The nurse came in and wanted to know from me if I had had any bowel movement. I didn't know what it meant, and I asked the nurse, "What's that?" Fred with his cigarette in his mouth muttered the words to me, "She wants to know if you had the shits yet." I started to laugh and had to press a pillow on my stomach because I was afraid that the stitches would burst. Finally I told the blushing nurse, "Not yet." A short time later I did have to go to the bathroom down the hallway. It was difficult for me to walk I moved my body in a painfully slow motion, finally arriving just in time. All the stalls were occupied except the one at the far end. I was lucky for as soon I sat down all that junk came out of me, stinking to high heaven. I heard the noise of toilet paper being unrolled in a real hurry followed by the sounds of flushing. As people were running out of the lavatory I heard a few of them say, "…oh, shit…" The horrible smell emptied the place in no time. I had a great laugh and at the same time felt great relief.

10

Linda Sue Ward

Meeting Linda Sue Ward

There was a Civil Service organization on base run by a nonmilitary person. This group was responsible for providing some form of entertainment for the troops and civilian employees on base. Among other things, one of their projects was to do staged Broadway musicals. The 36th Army Band supplied the musicians for the small pit orchestra. Since I played both the clarinet and the saxophone I was asked to play. The musical was "The Bells Are Ringing" (there were others also). During rehearsals with the cast, we musicians had a chance to see the action on stage and observe the actors and actresses. One actress caught my eyes. She stood out head and shoulders above the rest of the cast members.

This actress's portrayal of her character was very believable, and on top of that, she had a marvelous voice. It became obvious to me that I was listening to a well-trained musician. Her beautiful tone had warmth; the phrasing of musical lines accentuated the character she was presenting. She was beautiful on stage, and it was fun to watch her movements and facial expressions as she was delivering both her speaking and singing lines. After one of the rehearsals I was invited to join some of the cast for coffee in Sierra Vista. I went over to talk to the actress. She introduced herself as Linda Sue Ward. During our talks I learned that she was a teacher in an elementary school on base. She was from Tucson and graduated recently from the University of Arizona in education and voice. Her true love was singing and performing.

Linda and I started dating and performing together. We formed a trio that consisted of her singing, me playing the clarinet, and a piano accompanist. Linda and I were married, and we joined the Arizona Artists in Residence program as husband and wife, and performed in many places in Arizona. We also appeared on KUAT-TV a few times.

Citizen of the United States of America

One day I received orders to be shipped to Okinawa in thirty days. I was scared, for I wasn't a U.S. citizen and was afraid to leave the country for fear of not being able to come back. I went to see Colonel Fisher, asking him if anything could be done to delay my transfer until I became a U.S. citizen in a few months. This took place in the early 1962. I explained to him that I was eligible for citizenship; I had already turned in the required application forms and was waiting for a response and a date for my naturalization ceremony from the Immigration and Naturalization Service. I also told him that I would feel more comfortable going overseas as a U.S. citizen. He knew my background and he understood my concern. In a few weeks I received information from Washington, D.C., that my orders were to be delayed until I became a naturalized citizen.

Shortly after, the long-awaited letter from the Immigration and Naturalization Service arrived. I was to report at the courthouse in Bisbee, Arizona, on August 14, 1962, for the swearing-in ceremony. I was elated and so was Linda. (By this time we were living off-base in a trailer court in Huachuca City, Arizona). I had waited over five years for the honor of becoming a citizen of the United States. The notification packet included a study booklet; I was responsible for learning and being able to answer questions about the government of the U.S. and the state of Arizona. I had to know the three branches of government; names of the president, vice-president, speaker of the house; names of the officials in Arizona; term limits, etc.

Sergeant Jay "Pop" Brown, a career soldier and member of the army band, was to be my witness from the military. He was a wonderful, caring human being with an always-present, friendly smile. He was well read, was an intellectual, and played both the tuba and upright string bass well. He had a major weakness, one that he could not control or did not want to control. He was obsessed with alcohol, mainly beer, which he drank a lot of every night off base. I had never seen him drunk, because by the time he returned to the barracks after being in town, I was already long asleep. He did not have much sophistication; he would pass some of the most unbelievably rotten, foul-smelling gas in the middle of the barracks making us run to the closest open window for fresh air. He took a great deal of delight in this. There were many times when most of the toilet seats in the rest room were occupied with people reading the newspaper peacefully. When Sergeant Brown entered to use one of the empty seats one could hear the words, "Oh, shit" loud and clear while the whole washroom emptied in record-setting time. Although all the windows were wide open it took some time before it was safe to re-enter the bathroom again.

One day he invited me to join him for a beer at the bar. Soon I discovered what made him generate that incredibly foul smell. He loved to eat hard-boiled pickled eggs while drinking beer, producing that nasty sulfur-type smell. While having a few beers we had nice conversations on many occasions. He was a loner, but at the bar a totally different person. Everybody knew him and he knew each person by name; he was like a magnet, drawing people around himself. He was among friends there. He was well liked and easily approached. I liked him and he took a liking to me. A few weeks before my naturalization date I asked him if he would be my witness at the ceremony and if he would write a letter of recommendation on my behalf to be presented to the presiding judge. He told me that that was one of the greatest honors bestowed on him. I noticed a pair of teary eyes, which he tried to hide.

On Tuesday, August 14, 1962, he put on his best military uniform. I had never seen him dressed more sharply. He was walking tall, acting like a proud father. With Linda, the three of us drove about twenty miles to Bisbee, Arizona, for the 10:00 A.M. ceremony. On that day around noon I became a citizen of the United States of America. A long awaited dream of mine came through. That evening all of us bandsmen went to Sierra Vista to celebrate. I was as proud as I could be and the others were glad for my happiness. I'm sure I had a few drinks that night. In a matter of days, I received orders to be transferred to Germany.

The next time I saw Sergeant Brown was in Tucson at one of the VFW Posts on North Oracle Road. I found out that he had retired from the army and was residing in Tucson. We had a short visit at the VFW and we reminisced. A few months later I learned that he died in his sleep and his body wasn't discovered for more than a week. His friends at the VFW became concerned about his absence and they called the police, who made the discovery. That wonderful person died a loner, with no one around him. I miss him.

The next time I saw Dr. Jones, I told him about my transfer. He was sorry to hear the news, and asked me about my plans for the future after being discharged from the army. I told him about my plans, which were uncertain. I wanted to go back to Boston to continue my studies at the conservatory. However, the tuition was too steep even with a partial scholarship. He told me to keep in touch with him from Germany, and if I was interested in living in Tucson, he would see if he could get me a scholarship to the

University of Arizona. I thanked him for his offer; I told him that I would keep my options open and would keep in touch.

I said good-bye to the many friends I had made during my stay in the band and in Sierra Vista. I thanked Colonel Fisher for all his help and friendship. Interestingly enough, forty years later during one of my concerts with the Arizona Symphonic Winds at Udall Park, an elderly gentleman with a friendly smile that looked familiar came up to me during intermission and asked if I remembered him. It was Col. Robert Fisher. He told me how proud he and his wife were of me. They had just moved to the Tucson area and had seen my name in the newspaper. He told me that they were going to visit their children, but would be attending my concerts in the future on their return. I haven't seen them since and I wonder if they are still alive.

On to Germany

I wasn't very excited about going to Germany, especially when I found out my new orders were to Fulda, a city less than four miles from the East German border. East Germany was a communist-controlled country then, too close for comfort. Almost six years earlier I had escaped from the communist world known as the "Iron Curtain;" now I was heading back near to it. I was somewhat comforted knowing that I was going back as an American citizen and was in the military. Linda was excited; she had never been to Europe and was ready to travel and see different parts of the world. We started to pack. In my case it was very easy; all of my military clothing was in the duffle bag. Linda had a couple of suitcases to carry. We put everything into our '53 Chevy (actually it was her car) and drove to Boston to see my parents and have them meet their daughter-in-law for the first time.

Before leaving Boston we parked the Chevy in the garage where my parents lived. (They had to pay rent every month to have it parked there, something I didn't know until many years later.)

No Regrets

After a few days in Boston we took the train to New York City where I boarded the *USS Constitution*, a troop transport. Linda took an ocean liner to Europe. She was to land in Naples, Italy, after making visits to many ports on the way, and then take the train to Fulda. She was to arrive about two weeks after my arrival. I wasn't a tourist, she was.

My ship landed at the port of Bremerhaven, Germany, located on the North Sea. From there we took the train first to Frankfurt then to Fulda, where I had to report for duty in the Cavalry's 84th Army Band.

Upon arrival in Fulda I immediately reported to the building where the band was housed. The commanding officer's door was open and two men in soldier's uniforms seemed busy inside. One had to be the secretary for he was typing away; the other person was sitting at another desk that faced the open door. There was a nameplate that read "Master Sergeant Harrison." Sergeant Harrison was very much involved with reading military documents and didn't see me standing at the open door.

I decided to knock on the open door and when he looked up I said, "Sp4 Veres reporting for duty, sir." He looked at me knowing very well who I was, for one of the documents he was reading had my name on it. He kept looking at me. Finally he spoke, posing a totally unexpected question that floored me: "Do you play chess?" This I wasn't anticipating, but the secretary did, for in a swift move he turned around, waiting anxiously for my answer while displaying a sarcastic smile on his face.

When I was about nine years old, a real chess set was given to us children by our parents as a Christmas present. Speaking for myself, I was very happy to receive the set. The reason I say "real chess set" is because during the war years we played chess with figures that were made out of dough and dried in the oven. While I was buried deep in my thoughts reminiscing, I didn't realize that unconsciously I was uttering the words "I used to play" to which he immediately replied, "Good." With that said, he stood up, motioning to me to follow him. He was a small of stature, maybe 5'4" tall and very slender. He led me into the band/recreation room and told me to start setting up the chessboard, which was located next to the pool table. We started the game and in my nervousness I was moving too fast without thinking. I could have beaten him, but as it turned out we drew. He was impressed, because for the first time somebody gave him a challenge in a game that he loved.

Among the bandsmen the word spread in a hurry: Sergeant Harrison met his challenge. This became a blessing for me, for while others were scrubbing floors or were ready to go out in the middle of the night in full pack for the alert call, I was playing chess.

Being only a short distance from the Iron Curtain's border, alerts were regular features on this army base. I clearly remember one night when the siren went off and all of us had to put our gear on, ready to move out. I was quick in dressing and was the first one in line reporting. He told me to set up the chessboard and we started to play. We were in the middle of the game when the second siren went off and soldiers ran out of the building and lined up outside. I said to him with a nervous voice, "Sergeant, we have to go." To that he calmly replied, "Your move." Hours later when other soldiers were returning from the alert call we were still playing chess.

The more we played the better he got and so did I. However, I wanted to improve my playing. I bought myself a chess book and started to study openings and end-game problems. My chess game improved tremendously and I started to beat him regularly with ease. He could not understand what was happening; the harder he tried the worst he got. Of course I didn't tell him about my secret studies.

One day Linda was on base shopping in the commissary when she ran into Sergeant Harrison. The sergeant had an ear-to-ear smile on his face and for the first time he actually greeted my wife. Linda asked him about his good mood and to that he replied,

"I beat your husband in chess today." Linda told me that Sergeant Harrison was walking on cloud nine that day. She got a kick out of this and had a big laugh. Needless to say, he befriended me and that made my life comfortable until the day I left for the states.

Apartment living in Germany

Linda and I rented an apartment about four or five miles from the base and used the bus for transportation to get there every day. The winter in 1962-63 was the coldest in the century; even the Rhine River, which is the major waterway in Germany, froze, paralyzing the economy. Heating oil could not be shipped in and there was a shortage; however, oil was available to us Americans on base. I had a dilemma and had to solve it. Linda was seven or eight months pregnant and I had to find a way to get oil to the apartment stove to make her comfortable.

I purchased a five-gallon gasoline can and filled it up on base. I put the can in my duffle bag to hide it and tried to get on the bus, but the driver would not let me because of the fire danger. I went back to the base and purchased a bicycle that had a carrier in the back. I tied the can to it and started to pedal home in the freezing cold. There was snow on the ground that made my pedaling difficult, and on top of that, I had the heavy gasoline tank filled with oil tied to the rack that made the bike very unstable. The carrier rack wasn't designed to carry such a heavy item and I thought it would break any moment. The final mile to our apartment was all up hill and although I was in top physical condition I had to get off the bike to push it. The slippery snow made a cracking sound every time I took a step.

I finally got to the apartment totally exhausted but in good spirits, for we had oil. Very carefully I started to pour oil into the heating stove, trying very hard not to spill the precious liquid. Some oil did spill. I tried desperately to wipe off the excess oil but could not do it. I lit the stove and as it was heating up, the spilled oil created smoke. I rushed to the windows and opened them wide, letting the ice-cold air into the room. It took at least an hour to get rid of the smoke and finally we were able to close the windows to enjoy heat in the apartment for the first time. Linda was more than pleased and so was I.

Going to the bathroom was a shivering experience that winter. Those days in almost every home in Europe, the water tank was situated high above the toilet and a chain had to be pulled for a flush. We kept the bathroom door closed to keep as much of the heat in the bedroom as possible. Just before bedtime, Linda told me that the toilet wouldn't flush. I checked it out, and sure enough I couldn't pull the chain either. I put some chairs on top of each other and climbed up to the water tank. When I looked inside, a block of ice was staring at me. To flush, water had to be heated on the stove, poured into the tank, and then we had to wait for the ice to melt. Pouring water directly into the toilet from the bucket was the fast way to flush, but it needed the force from the elevated tank to flush down the "dump." Lovely memories.

To fight the outside cold temperatures I would have a tall glass of steaming hot tea with a large dose of rum in it every morning before I left for the base. If it worked in the long run, I don't know; however, I was warm until I got to the bus stop at 6:00 A.M. I danced in place until the public bus showed up. The bus was not heated, but all the people on the way to work standing like a bunch of sardines gave us warmth. I would take the bicycle to work only when I needed to bring back oil for the stove.

After my first experience with pouring oil into the stove, the next day I bought a funnel and from that day on not a drop was wasted. Our apartment became cozy and we even left the bathroom door open to avoid shivering in there and to be able to flush. Our child was on its way, and we wanted to have a warm apartment for the baby.

No Regrets

Michael Veres

February 11, 1963, started out like a typical day following the regular day-to-day pattern: waking up at 5:00 A.M.; getting dressed; drinking the hot tea with rum; saying good-bye to Linda; walking down the hill to the bus stop while freezing; going to the army base to perform the daily routine of rehearsing, practicing, and chess-playing with Sergeant Harrison. By this time I was beating him about nine out of ten times. Although it seemed like just another routine day, it was slightly different. That morning Linda stayed in bed complaining about some stomach cramps, but told me not to worry, for they would go away shortly. Little did I know what was taking place.

At the army base after roll call we had some free time before rehearsal started and Sergeant Harrison wanted to play chess. We had made just a few moves when he asked me about Linda's condition. I told him that this morning she was talking about some slight stomach cramps. At that point he jumped up, ran into his office, and was on the phone calling the military ambulance service. He sent me down to the already waiting ambulance and told me to go home and get my wife to the hospital in a hurry, for most likely she was having labor pains.

It took no time to reach the apartment with the siren on. I ran upstairs with the two other medics and told Linda that we were going to the 97th U.S. Army General Hospital located in Frankfurt, one of the major cities in Germany. Her reply was that she was feeling better. We got her in the ambulance, with me sitting next to her as she was lying in bed, while one of the medics was checking her blood pressure, etc. The road was bumpy and she was complaining about being uncomfortable. I told her that it was only about a forty-mile drive and we would be there soon.

At the hospital they checked her in and the officer in charge told me to get back to my base for non-patients were not allowed to stay on the premises. I took the train back, and in the band barracks a message was waiting for me. I looked at the memo that said, "…false labor, but the hospital will keep her overnight for observation."

Next day during rehearsal as Sergeant Harrison was conducting the band, the secretary walked in with a memo in his hand, handing it over to him. He glanced at it, stopped the rehearsal, and with a loud voice made the announcement, "It's a boy! Mother and child are doing well." On February 12, 1963, Michael Veres was born and I became a father. I was flying high as a kite in a good windy day, enjoying tremendous happiness in my life. Next morning I took the train to Frankfurt.

The baby was wrapped in warm blankets as we left the hospital to catch the train back to Fulda. I was holding our newborn son tightly to my body, the most precious thing on earth, showering him with kisses. Linda was still very weak from giving birth and had difficulty walking. Since she was doing fine, the hospital released her to make room for other expectant mothers. On the train many German ladies were making remarks to me about keeping the child warm. Because of the very cold temperature they were concerned for the child's safety. We arrived in Fulda in the late evening, holding on to Michael and being very careful not to fall on the slippery, snow-covered street. After the bus ride we were in the apartment. One of the suitcases became Michael's first bed. He was a good little baby, waking only when he was hungry.

I washed the diapers by hand in the bathtub, drying them in the kitchen/living room next to the stove on a piece of string crossing the room. Michael started exercising early in his life, pushing himself up with his hands, holding his head up while looking around the room. Four weeks later we took him to the medical facilities on base where he received a bunch of shots to get him ready to enter the United States. I held him during the procedure trying to keep him calm. He was crying and I cried along with him as he was receiving the needles. In the middle of March, Linda and Michael boarded the plane to Boston, and eventually to

Tucson to meet both sets of his grandparents. I still had five more months to go before discharge. I gave up the apartment, and moved back into the army barracks.

My father loved children and Michael was no exception. Looking at photographs one can clearly see the radiant faces of my parents as they were holding their first grandchild. The same goes for Linda's parents, Ruth and Ira Ward, two very beautiful people who loved him to death.

László's parents with baby Michael, 1963

Michael with his mother, Linda, 1963

Linda Sue Ward

Michael attended Marshall Elementary School for the first and second grades, and then transferred to Gale Elementary after we purchased our newly-built house in a new subdivision on East 29th Street in 1970. Linda still lives in that house. When the time arrived he joined the beginning band at his elementary school playing the clarinet. He stayed with the band programs until his graduation from high school.

The house was in the Santa Rita school area, future high school for Mike. At first I didn't want him to be in my band; I didn't want him to see how his dad, a teacher, had to handle the unruly students in his classes, but I changed my mind. The unruly students were very few and far between. We drove to school together having good times while doing it. He joined the band playing the clarinet, eventually switching to the tuba. He progressed rapidly and made Regional Honor Band every year.

While at Secrist Junior High, he became interested in track and field extracurricular activities. His passion was throwing the shot and discus. In high school he continued track and field under the guidance of Larry Williams, a biology teacher and an excellent coach for shot put, discus throwers, and others. In his senior year Michael was Arizona State champion in the discus event! What a marvelous way to finish up his high school years!

Although I had a very busy schedule, Mike and I took lots of trips together in his younger years to California to visit my side of the family. We went to Disneyland and Magic Mountain, and also to Florida. I would put a mattress in the back of the VW hatchback where he would sleep through the night while I was driving. Nine hours later when I parked the car in front of my brother Zoli's house Mike would get up and say, "We are here already?" Just for the record, Mike is a big Redskins fan. I love Mike dearly and I love his beautiful family.

Today, Mike is married to Karyn (Missy), his high school sweetheart, and they have two beautiful girls, Kayleen and Karylin. I'm a proud grandfather. They live on two acres of land on the northwest part of Tucson with their numerous animals. Because of Mike's work ethic, he is the owner, with his wife, of a successful restaurant called "Cibaria," a feat accomplished by pure, gutsy, hard work. Mike is one of the most respected chefs in the business and an artist in the field of gourmet cooking. I'm extremely proud of his achievements.

Michael accepts a check for his athletic achievements, 1981

Gourmet chef Michael, his wife Karyn, and their children, Kayleen (standing) and Karylin, 1999. Michael and Karyn own the very successful Cibaría.

Linda Sue Ward

The beginning of my conducting career

The great amount of practicing I was doing on the clarinet finally took its toll. One of my front teeth got so loose from the steady pressure that it had to be pulled. The doctors were going to give me a removable plate, but I put up a good fight asking for a bridge so I could continue my career as a clarinet player. They told me the cost of the bridge was too high and the military would not approve of it. I told them that it happened during my time in the military. The dentist felt sorry for me and cared about my future. He made up a report that my teeth problem was caused during one of the military exercises, attaching the blame to some unknown source. I received my bridge about six weeks later and still remember his words: "Take a good look at this bridge; it is paid for by the taxpayers." I thanked him and slowly I was back practicing again.

Sergeant Harrison conducted most of the band rehearsals while the band's commanding officer very seldom ran the practice sessions except for special occasions. Sgt. Harrison was a very nice person, at least to me. However, his musicianship was very limited and so was his conducting. I think he played the flute, but he never did while I was there. His main duty was to run the administrative part of the organization. One day during rehearsal he was called out for an important phone call. "Who would like to take over while I'm gone?" he asked, but before he could finish the sentence my hand went up. He handed me the baton and without knowing what I was doing I started up the band. I had a good time and after the rehearsal the musicians applauded me. I ran many rehearsals after that day, gaining much experience in being in front of a group while developing my musical knowledge and conducting technique in the process.

While in Germany the band traveled a lot, performing many parades in many cities including Bonn, Dresden, Essen, Kassel, and Dusseldorf. While in Bonn, capital city of West Germany, I

No Regrets

made sure that I visited the birthplace of Beethoven on 16 Bonn Gasse (Bonn Street), right next to a park where his statue is erected. The building is a simple two-story house turned into a museum. Since it was Sunday when I visited, the building was closed, but I made certain that I touched the door where the great master entered and exited many times.

One day we were informed that the president of the United States, John F. Kennedy, was to visit Berlin with a short stopover Frankfurt. The band spent much time in perfecting marches, especially Sousa's "Thunderer." We were taken to Frankfurt where we were to join many other bands for a massed band. I remember there were sixty-four trumpets which produced lots of sound. We were assembled at the military airport waiting in typical military fashion; that is, hurry up and wait.

Finally a helicopter became visible, then another and another. They were circling the field while we were trying to guess which one had the president in it. Finally one of the choppers landed and one of the black limousines standing by with the presidential flag pulled up. No one got into that limo. Another helicopter landed and this time it was the president. He got into the open-top limo, and the driver slowly approached as the band was playing the "Thunderer." I was standing in the front row. Just at the time when the limo was almost before us, all sixty-four trumpets hit the bugle call section of the march, sending chills down my spine. I shall never forget that sunny spring day in Frankfurt. That young-looking president was waving at us with a big smile on his face, promising an incredible future for generations to come. I felt he was waving at me only. A few months later he was killed by an assassin's bullet.

I kept up my correspondence with Dr. Wendall Jones about the possible scholarship at the University of Arizona. In May I received an official letter from the university confirming a full music scholarship for the 1963-64 school year. The scholarship was to be automatically renewed for the next four years as long as I maintained a C average. Before Linda returned to the states with

Linda Sue Ward

Michael, we had discussed the possible scholarship I might receive. Since I had a trade and a family, I felt responsible to support them by working as an automobile mechanic. In my mind the husband's duty was to take care of his family financially, and that I intended to do. Linda's opinion was that I should go to school and get my degree. During that time she was willing to work as a teacher to support the family. We were going back and forth on this subject until I gave in and decided to go to school if the scholarship did come through.

I signed the scholarship document and returned it via certified mail to the university.

11

To Tucson

Getting discharged from military service

It was customary among the band people to take a "short timer" to town for a few drinks. Two days before my departure it was my turn. We visited many beer halls, had a beer here and there, and ate good German bratwursts between drinks. We all had a good time until the alcohol hit me. We were in a car driving to another beer joint. I was in the back seat when suddenly the whole world started to turn and my head spun. I told the driver to stop the car and as soon as I opened the back door, I leaned out and emptied the contents of my stomach on the street. That was the first and last time for me to have so much to drink. Next morning I had a major headache and my head was constantly spinning. Luckily it was a Sunday and a duty-free day, so I had plenty of time to recover before the 6:30 A.M. roll call on Monday morning.

It was time to say my good-byes again to the many nice people I had met. Sergeant Harrison and I hugged each other and he wished me well. We played one more game of chess for old times' sake, and if I remember correctly, he won the game. By that time I didn't care.

To Tucson

I took the train to Bremerhaven where I boarded the troop carrier ship with thousands of others to return to the United States. Another chapter in my life was slowly coming to a close and an unforeseen future was waiting for me. I was looking forward to seeing my parents and brothers again and could hardly wait to see Linda and Michael also.

The ship crossed the Atlantic in five days and docked in New York City. I walked off the ship as a civilian with an honorable discharge in my hands. It was good to be a civilian again; on the other hand there was sadness. I was proud to have served three years in the military. I did my duty as a citizen and was ready to go back in case there was a war and the military needed me. I gained much growth during my tenure in the service and I became a better person because of that. I didn't realize how much good the military did for me until I became a classroom teacher.

Doing my duty in the military was a small price to pay for the privilege of coming to America and eventually becoming a citizen of the greatest country in the world.

At the time of my discharge I was twenty-six years old. It was 1963.

On to Tucson; the beginning of my undergraduate years at the University of Arizona

After spending a few days in Boston it was time to move on to Tucson. The '53 Chevy was running smoothly in the early hours as I headed to west. I couldn't wait to see my family in Tucson. Almost six months had gone by since I had seen Linda and Michael. I drove non-stop to St. Louis where I rested overnight. Next morning I was on my way, arriving in Tucson in the early hours. Traveling by car from Boston made me realize how large this country was.

After temporarily settling down at Linda's parents' home, I was ready to start at the university right after Labor Day. Michael

No Regrets

had grown a lot; he wasn't a tiny little baby anymore. Linda's parents, Ira and Ruth Ward, were very warm and friendly towards their new son-in law. They were beautiful people and especially Ira Ward, who would do anything to help. He and his wife were down-to-earth, extremely unselfish people. I shall always think of them with nice thoughts. They loved Michael to death and were built-in baby sitters. Linda started teaching at Sam Hughes Elementary School, while I, without realizing what was going on, started my college education as a freshman.

Since I had no high school diploma I was admitted by the University of Arizona under the classification of "special student" meaning that for the first five semesters I was not a candidate for a college degree. After the five semesters, the counseling department would review my grades for evaluation. If the grades were a C average, I could become a candidate for a degree.

After the assessment I officially became a candidate for a music education degree. I finished all my required courses in three-and-a-half years and graduated with distinction. During my undergraduate years I had only one goal in my mind: receive a degree as fast as possible, and get some kind of job to support my family.

I had no idea what an education degree was all about at the time. I didn't know that I was becoming a future teacher. Now I'm thankful for my counseling professor who guided me in that direction.

One incident during my senior year sticks out clearly. I was taking a low string class with Professor Sammarco. For the final test we students had to come up with a lesson plan and teach it to the class. My turn came and I did my teaching. Was it any good? I didn't know. I was the last one to leave the classroom and outside the door Prof. Anita Sammarco was talking to a colleague. From the distance I heard her voice, "There goes a born teacher." Since there was no one around she must have been talking about me. I'll never forget those words; it gave me an incredible boost and from

To Tucson

that moment on, there was no question about my future in the field of music. A teacher I would be, even though I loved my clarinet. As it turned out a few years later, I did both. I had the best of two worlds in my profession.

Prior to registration I had to take a proficiency test in English for placement. To my surprise I was placed in English 101 while many others failed and had to sign up for a refresher course. After a few sessions in that class I realized that I didn't belong there and transferred to an English class that was offered for foreign students like me. My vocabulary was limited and the English that I learned in the army wasn't spoken at the school of higher education. I had a very difficult time in classes like sociology and psychology, because of my language limitation. I carried a dictionary with me at all times, constantly looking up words I had never heard nor seen before. It was a slow, painful process, but I was learning. Writing term papers was a nightmare and so were exams.

Needless to say, I failed both sociology and psychology. I was totally lost. I never bothered to retake the class in sociology; the subject matter was totally uninteresting to me at that time. Today, with more knowledge of the English language under my belt, a class like that would be fun to take. Since I had to have a science class for graduation, I took psychology over again in summer school and passed. Because the class was retaken within the first year, the failing grade was taken off from my transcripts.

During summer school older people attended classes and they knew how to study for tests. They formed study groups and I was invited to join in the study sessions. I passed the class with a high grade, thanks to those nice people. They were patient with me, were willing to help me along the way, and in the process my English vocabulary increased at a fast rate.

In music classes I was doing very well. Being older then ninety-nine percent of the freshmen, my musical background put me way ahead of most students in my classes. I spent a great deal of time practicing my clarinet and between classes the place to

No Regrets

find me was in one of the practice rooms.

The time came to audition for chair placement for the Symphonic Band (that was the top band those days). Professors Jack Lee and Dr. Sam Fain were judging the clarinets. The audition involved a solo work and some sight-reading. The sight-reading portion was the "Tarantella" section from Tchaikovsky's "Capriccio Italien" composition. I felt good about my audition. Since I wasn't in marching band I didn't know any of the other players. However, they knew each other and had a good idea how the order of the clarinet section would be. There was tremendous disappointment on many faces when the results were posted and questions were asked all around, not just from clarinet players but from other instrumentalists: who is László Veres? During my tenure at the university, I held the principal clarinet position in both band and orchestra, and due to my playing ability, my scholarship was renewed year after year. At that point in my life, there is no way I could have attended a university without financial help. I'm grateful to professors Wendall Jones, Jack Lee, and above all to my wife, Linda, for talking me into being a student and for her willingness to work as a teacher during my days as a student.

I well recall the words of Felix Viscuglia, my teacher at the New England Conservatory, "If you are good, everybody wants you. No one wants somebody who is average." The hard work, sweat, and total dedication to bettering myself were paying off handsomely for me.

About thirty years later I presented a special "Tribute to Jack Lee" concert by performing musical compositions written by him. This was my way of paying homage to the man who provided a scholarship for me; who was my professor and band director at the university; and to recognize and honor this wonderful human being. After the concert he sent me the following note:

Dear László,
    As I started to Thank You for the wonderful tribute you gave me…my thoughts are not about me and my music, but of the great

admiration I have for you and the sincerity of your work. While you give me credit for my little works that I have achieved in my career I want you to know that no one in Arizona is respected as a musician (and a Super Conductor) more than you, plus you are liked. As a person you have real balance, far above the average music educator. When you conducted my "A Dance from a Dream," it was done with great feeling. Yours is a great gift (very rare)...In our business Emotion separates the men from the boys...

I was deeply touched by Jack Lee's letter and shall always treasure his words.

Musical experiences at the School of Music

The time had arrived for the Symphonic Band's first rehearsal. The director of bands was Jack Lee. The Symphonic Band was made up of graduate students and upper classmen. Most likely I was the only freshman, but again, I was four to five years older than most of them. After playing a march or something for a warm up, Lee called out the next piece, "Rhapsody in Blue," by Gershwin. In this piece the opening calls for the famous glissando (sliding) solo played by the clarinet. (I had studied this with Viscuglia in Boston and also practiced it many times; it wasn't new to me, but was totally new to most of the players in the band.) After the downbeat given by the conductor to the band, I went into my trill, slowly sliding up the scale, accelerating, and finally slowly pulling the glissando to the high C. Lee brought the band in too early and I said to him, "Mr. Lee, would you please wait for me until I finish my glissando." By this time the drop of a needle could have been heard in the band room. All eyes were on me, and I saw many dropped jaws. I did my solo again and this time the band entered at the right time after the conductor's cue. My reputation as a clarinet player was established among the players of the band. By the second rehearsal, "Rhapsody in Blue" was taken out of the folders.

Every Thursday during lunch hour there were student recitals held in the music school's auditorium and every music student was required to attend. Performing these recitals was strictly on a volunteer basis; all a participant had to have was the professor's recommendation. I signed up at the very first opportunity and by the second month of the first semester I was put on the recital list. Most of the performers were from the piano, voice, and string departments, and they were mostly juniors and seniors. I was only a freshman and the only performer not from the mentioned departments. I had an advantage over most of the students however, because I was several years older than most of them, and with a lot more performing experience. The program for every week was posted on the preceding Monday on the bulletin board in the hallway for everyone to see. When I saw my name listed I became very nervous; I didn't expect to be picked so early in the school year.

The University of Arizona student in 1965, age 27

With great anticipation on my part the big day finally arrived. Curiosity brought many of the professors to the auditorium that day wanting to find out more about this clarinetist who was about to perform a composition by Stravinsky. Among the profes-

To Tucson

sors attending was Russell Sherman from the piano department. After my performance, he hurried backstage to congratulate me, told me how impressed he was, and wanted to know if I ever played the piece called "Contrasts," by Bartók. The piece was totally unknown to me. He said that it was a trio, calling for violin, clarinet and piano, one of the great works in the repertoire. He was willing to teach and coach this composition to talented players if there was interest. One of his graduate students would be the pianist, another student on violin, and me on clarinet. As violinist he suggested Steve Folks, who had just been discharged from the military where he was a member of the famous Seventh Army Symphony Orchestra in Europe. He was a freshman just like me and close to my age. Steve was an outstanding violinist and was very much interested in the project.

"Contrasts" is one of the most difficult compositions. It was highly demanding technically for each of the players. Personally, I put in many hours of hard work learning it as did the others, truly enjoying the challenge. Then came the most difficult part of them all: putting the ensemble together under Russell Sherman's coaching, molding the three of us into one unit. After many rehearsals we were put on the Thursday's student recital. We brought the house down. They had never heard anything like that before. Wendall Jones, my clarinet teacher, was in the audience and was very impressed. He had a short conversation with Russell Sherman after the performance.

Soon we found out what was going on. The Music Educational National Conference was to be held in Long Beach, California in the spring, and one of the clinicians was to be Wendall Jones. He wanted to know if our trio could perform "Contrasts" as part of his lecture presentation. We agreed to do it. We kept working on improving our ensemble to play for this important performance.

The day came for our presentation. The room was a typical classroom, with student desks and chairs. As we were setting up, music educators were slowly entering the room to hear Professor

Jones' lecture. Our turn came and we dug into our musical composition with total concentration and focus on our music. After the first movement I happened to look up and could not believe what was happening. There were people standing in every available inch of the room, some even standing on chairs at the back of the room for a better view. At the end of the Finale, there was an outburst of "bravos" that went on for a several minutes. I had never experienced anything like that before or since. Our trio put the University of Arizona Music department on the map, thanks to the vision and trust of professors Russell Sherman and Wendall Jones.

While rehearsing, I found out that Russell Sherman was a world-class concert pianist, one of the finest, and was just hired by the university as a full professor. He was young, friendly, and energetic. When he found out that I had lived in Boston, studied at the New England Conservatory, and was a Celtics fan, we became friends. We had coffee many times, and talked about many things, basketball being one of them. He stayed at the university only about two years, for he was way too talented for Tucson, and as soon as he received the offer from the New England Conservatory to be head of the piano department there, he left the university. I was sad to see him go. I lost a good friend, an incredible artist. On the other hand it was a tremendous opportunity for him. I kept hearing him on radio broadcasts performing piano concertos with some of the world's great orchestras. I wish him well.

Other activities while a student

While working as a full-time teacher, Linda was also a member of the music school's Opera Company, Musical Theater, and years later, of the Arizona Opera Company and Southern Arizona Light Opera Company (SALOC). She kept up her singing with lessons from the famous baritone, Igor Gorin, who after retiring from the Metropolitan Opera House, taught at the university. Linda had a beautiful soprano voice; she was great in both opera and

To Tucson

musical theater. She moved with grace on stage and her facial expressions were priceless. She did marvelous jobs in creating the main roles in "Hello Dolly," "The King and I," and "Sound of Music." With the opera company she had the leading roles in "Tosca," "Dido and Aeneas," "Marriage of Figaro," and many others. Linda has a twin sister, also a soprano, who did some studying in Europe and performed there for a while. Linda always thought that her sister Martha was much better than she was, and idolized her. In my opinion, Linda had a better voice, with much more expression, and more convincing in her delivery. I told her that numerous times but she wouldn't listen and that frustrated me. By constantly "playing second fiddle" to her sister, she never developed the much-needed confidence this business requires.

Besides carrying a full load of studies during my student years, I was holding part-time jobs. Tuesday and Thursday evenings I worked at a liquor store in Campbell Plaza (Campbell and Glenn); while Saturdays and Sundays were spent at a gas station on the corner of Kolb and Broadway. In the middle of the 1960s Broadway and Kolb were two-lane streets.

What about Michael? The grandparents took care of him most of the time. I wish I could have spent more time with him in his early years.

At the end of my third year at the university, Robert Vagner was in Tucson visiting friends while conducting the Arizona All-State Band. He was from the University of Oregon where he was professor of clarinet and director of bands. Dr. Jones introduced me to him and I played for him. He offered me a teaching-assistant position with pay while working on my master's degree in Eugene, Oregon. Linda and I talked about the offer and we moved up to Oregon and lived in the student housing for married couples. Linda was teaching the Head Start program and Mike was making friends in the neighborhood. His best friend's name was Joseph, but he pronounced it "Jofasz." (If the first two letters are taken away, the remaining word in Hungarian means penis). I always got a big kick out of it and had many good laughs.

Bob Vagner was a very fine clarinet teacher and an outstanding band director. His bands were highly respected in the Northwest area. In Oregon my teaching duties included teaching first-year clarinet students and clarinet instrumental classes for future teachers. During the fall semester I was doing my student teaching that was required for the bachelor's degree, while taking classes towards my master's degree. At the end of the fall semester my course work was completed for my required Bachelor of Music in Education degree, and I graduated with distinction from the University of Arizona in absentia, in December 1966. I was very proud and so were Linda and my parents. I was the first and still the only son who earned a college degree.

The summer of 1967 arrived and I was one class short of my master's degree. I received a job offer as band director in the small town of Tombstone, Arizona.

12

The Tucson Symphony Orchestra

The start of my teaching career and the Tucson Symphony Orchestra

While many others believed that Tombstone was a fictional place that existed only on TV or western movies, I was familiar with the town. Fort Huachuca was only about twenty miles from Tombstone and while in the army band there, we visited the town and marched in their annual "Helldorado" parade held in October. Linda had a desire to move back to Arizona and so did I. While in Oregon I applied and interviewed for middle and high school jobs in both Oregon and Washington states. While my interviews went well, or at least I thought they did, the repeated comment I received was, "We'll call you." Of course the calls never came, except for one from Professor Jack Lee, band director at the University of Arizona. He told me about the open teaching position for band director in Tombstone. I called the school district and they sent me some information about the town and the high school. I also received a letter from a person named Jerry Bowell. He introduced himself and told me that he was the choral director in the Tombstone schools and went on to say great things

No Regrets

about the students, parents, school, and the town. He did a good sales job on Linda and me, and the decision was made. After so many failed interviews it was great to have a job offer.

About the same time I also received a phone call from Wendall Jones telling me about the opening for the principal clarinet position in the Tucson Symphony. Tucson is about eighty-five miles from Tombstone, about one and one-half hours' drive, not too far to travel. Linda was excited; she was always hoping that one day I would play clarinet in that orchestra. She was also excited about being close to Tucson; she could visit her parents and take voice lessons at the university again. After being in Eugene, Oregon, for about a year, I packed the U-Haul trailer, hitched it to the good old '53 Chevy and headed south to Arizona. I was to return to Eugene during the next summer to complete my course work for the master's degree. Linda and Michael flew back to Tucson a few weeks earlier to avoid the long drive and also to look for housing in Tombstone.

Before driving to Tombstone, I stopped in Tucson and without any practicing in the past week I auditioned for the clarinet opening. I barely made the appointed date and hour. The audition took place at the Tucson Symphony office and Maestro Gregory Millar, conductor of the orchestra, listened to the applicants. That day there were about six of us that auditioned, two of them being doctoral students at the university. The audition process was to go on for a few days. I had no idea how many others were trying out for the vacancy. I had to play a solo and sight-read an excerpt from the symphonic literature. The sight-reading excerpt was from "Till Eulenspiegel" by Strauss. Thanks to Felix Viscuglia, I did well on that portion of my playing because I had studied it while at New England. I remember him telling me, "You should know some of the major solo works for clarinet, but let's study excerpts from the orchestral literature because that is where the money is." How right he was!

That same afternoon Maestro Millar called me into his

The Tucson Symphony Orchestra

office and offered me the principal clarinet position for the upcoming season. He mentioned that while my playing wasn't the best, he was going with me because of Wendall Jones' high recommendation. He showed concern about my commuting to the rehearsals and concerts from Tombstone. I told him that I was a hard worker and he wouldn't be sorry for choosing me. I couldn't wait to tell Linda the news. I was flying high for I had the best of everything going for me: I had a paying job as band director; appointed principal clarinetist with the symphony, and had my family. The next day we left for Tombstone and moved into a four-bedroom house about five blocks away from the high school. All this happened during the latter part of August 1967.

Tombstone years

We settled into our new home a few weeks before the first day of school. I spent much time in the high school band room organizing uniforms and music, getting ready for opening day. The building was an old army barracks converted to a classroom. There were windows on the east side; the west side windows were boarded up and bars were used to protect the building from the flying footballs, since the football field was situated right behind the building. The goal post was set about ten yards away from the band room.

In the north end of the band room there was a small old-fashioned iron stove equipped with a stovepipe. I had to be very careful not to put musicians too close to the stove when it was heated. During the winter months I would arrive early to start the fire in the stove, to make the room bearable in the cold mornings. I would put some newspaper in bottom of the stove followed with some kindling wood and eventually some coal. I had everything under control as far as the heating was concerned. Things were just like back in the old country and to build a fire in the stove was no big deal. I did it plenty of times in our apartment in Budapest.

No Regrets

The building had a thin roof, and when the sun came up, the temperature rose rapidly. During warm days the opened windows provided cooler air. The administration never heard a word of complaint from me on this matter.

I was as happy as one could be and considered myself to be a lucky person: I had a job, and I was to have my own high school band. Now it was up to me to prove myself in the field of teaching.

After spending some time in the band room I would go outside and kick some footballs on the field. I was doing some punting but mainly kicking field goals. One day I was in good form and was putting the ball between the uprights with regularity from the forty, forty-five and even from the fifty-yard lines. Two men were looking in from the main road through the fence and I recognized one of them as Jerry Stamp, principal at the junior high school. They were talking and watching me at the same time. Since I had an audience, I started to kick even better.

Later that day Jerry looked me up and told me about the other man, a Mr. Arnold, manager of the local bank and member of the school board. Arnold was known to be totally against music programs in the schools, for students who were involved with music were nothing but a bunch of "sissies" in his opinion. He was extremely outspoken on the subject and at board meetings constantly tried to argue his case. He was very interested in finding out who the kicker was on the field. Jerry couldn't wait to answer, "He is our new band director and he was a member of the Hungarian national soccer team." After that, Arnold didn't say a word and departed. By the time school had started I had all three of his children enrolled in the band program.

There was a welcoming get-together scheduled for all teachers provided by the superintendent, school board, and some important parents in the community. I was introduced to Mr. Arnold, who was extremely polite and friendly towards me. One lady parent came by, grabbed me by the arm, and led me away to meet her husband. While walking she told me what a first-class b___ Arnold was and warned me to stay away from him. I had received my first dose of small town gossip in a real hurry. They introduced themselves as Betty and Major Dale Patterson.

Betty asked me, "Honey, do you drink?" To that I shyly replied, "No, ma'am." She went on, "Honey, let me tell you something: by the time you leave Tombstone, you will be an alcoholic." Later on I found out what was happening in Tombstone. Almost every weekend there was a party given in somebody's home with plenty of alcoholic drinks on the premises. There wasn't much to do in Tombstone on the weekends. The big social gathering for the city folks took place on Friday nights during football season. The whole week's gossip was passed around while much drinking was taking place in the stands. I have to admit that I never saw alcoholic beverages being used, although I heard about it; and not once was there any kind of rude or nasty behavior displayed in the stands by anyone. As far as attending these parties, playing with the Tucson Symphony gave me good excuses not to show up. Those party people at first were disappointed with Linda and me for turning down their invitations. However, as time went by those people felt honored when we had some free time and accepted their invitations. As time went by, we ultimately became very good friends with Betty and Dale Patterson and kept our friendship for a long time, even after our departure from Tombstone.

Instrumental music in Tombstone

After Labor Day in 1967 school started and I was to face my first class of the day, the high school band. There were about thirty-two students in the band. The music I had passed out was simple stuff; at least that is what I thought. While in Eugene doing my student teaching, I had the chance to work with the finest high school band of the city, and in Tombstone I was expecting the players to have some kind of ability as did the bandsmen in Eugene. When I gave my first downbeat for a simple march, a rude awakening took place for me, the newly appointed director of bands. Within a few minutes I received my very first ice-cold shower in my teaching career. I put my baton down, looked around my new surroundings with all those faces staring at me. As I closed my eyes, a big sign brilliantly shone front of me: "Welcome to the teaching profession, Mr. László Veres."

We had to start on square one and it was up to me to move them ahead. At first I was ready to give up and was all set to throw in the towel. "Come on, László Veres, you are not going to give up that easily. You are a teacher and your job is to teach those young people. Have patience and faith in what you are doing," I was telling myself. Suddenly I felt energized and with new vigor and determination I was ready to take on the challenge. Within a few weeks we were on the football field marching in formations playing simple tunes fairly well. I was excited about what was happening and the excitement rubbed off on my students.

By late October the Tombstone Marching Band was competing at "Band Day" at the University of Arizona football stadium in Tucson. Band Day is a competition for marching bands from all over the state. We received a decent rating at Band Day. By the end of the school year the Tombstone High Concert Band received its very first "Superior" rating at the state-sponsored music festival held at the University of Arizona. Things were happening.

My other assignments included a fifth grade beginning band; sixth grade intermediate band, and a combined seventh and eighth grade band. At the elementary school I also had to teach third and fourth grades where the students learned to play the recorder. The junior high students had to walk over to the high school's band room for band rehearsal, while I had to travel to the elementary school where we practiced on the stage of a combination auditorium/cafeteria. Today they call it an MPR—Multi-Purpose Room. The distances for travel were not great.

The junior high band by the second year of my tenure was over eighty strong; not bad, considering that the junior high school

The Tucson Symphony Orchestra

had just over 100 students. Woody Parker, a drummer, liked to mess around in this band. His reading of musical notations at first was almost non-existent and his drumming was more like banging. I found out that in every other class he was a troublemaker, giving a hard time to all of his teachers. Woody spent more time in the principal's office being whacked than in the classroom. In those days teachers were allowed to spank an unruly child. Above the blackboard in the band room there was a spanking paddle hanging with "education board" painted on it in large letters for everyone to see. It was there most likely since the day school opened years ago. I seldom used it; didn't have to, for I could raise my voice to a scary level and that was enough to put a student on his/her best behavior in a hurry. When it was used, I always said that a good whack on the behind would send the brain upstairs where it belonged in no time.

Woody was one of the many students who were raised by a single mother. He loved band and had a great respect for me. He was first in the band room and the last one to leave. Many times I had to throw him out of the band room and would escort him to his next class.

One day in band he was totally out of control and I sent him to my office, telling him that I would deal with him at the end of rehearsal. With the "education board" in my hand I opened the door in my office and there was Woody on his knees, his closed eyes facing up to heaven, and mumbling a prayer. I had a difficult time holding back my laugh. I had never seen anything like that before. "What a creative mind this person has," I thought to myself. In a stern voice I told him to get out of there. He left my office faster than a bullet. During the spring concert Woody presented me with a drum stick that was almost three feet long, hand carved by him in perfect proportions. I always treasured that gift and it hung in my office for many years. He didn't want me to forget about him, and now, over thirty years later, I still think of him with warm thoughts. By the time I left Tombstone he was a totally

No Regrets

changed, well-behaved person, and for the first time in my teaching career I realized what the power of music is capable of. The last I heard, Woody had become a successful businessman.

Drummers are a bunch of highly energized people. Once they have a pair of sticks in their hands they will be put into motion. During rehearsal the band director might stop the band to correct mistakes; however, drummers will totally ignore it and will continue to do their thing. It was a long battle with the drummers, but eventually they got used to me and stopped playing when I stopped the band.

One day I was pushing the band hard during rehearsal; I was all business. There was no time for messing around. At one point I stopped the band and one of the drummers didn't stop. I picked up the eraser from the blackboard and threw it at him. The whole band ducked behind their stands and so did the drummer at the very last second. The eraser was well thrown and was right on target until he dodged it, barely missing him. The eraser flew right by his ears, breaking one of the windowpanes. When I left Tombstone, the drummers would not let the school engineer fix the broken window for a long time. The broken window had a special meaning for them. I was told later that the drummers were proud of the fact that it was Mr. Veres who broke the window and to them it was sacred. During the cold winter months the students would cover the window with a piece of cardboard, uncovering it during the warmer days. I guess the window wasn't repaired until some of those students graduated. I felt honored.

I would eat my lunch in the elementary school cafeteria just after the beginning band class three times a week. Marge Kernen, a very funny lady with a great personality, was running the kitchen staff. As always, I was first in line to be served for I had to get back to the high school for the afternoon classes. Fried chicken was on the menu that day, and as Marge was serving she asked me what part of the chicken would I like. I told her that I would like two pieces of chest, to which she cracked up laughing

The Tucson Symphony Orchestra

and could not stop. She couldn't wait to tell Linda and the other faculty members. As of this day Linda still gets a big chuckle out of that incident. This was the talk of the town for the longest time.

One day I asked Marge in German, "Wie geht es Ihnen?" (How are you?) Her reply was, "My gate needs to be painted."

On the football field I would combine all the junior high band members with the high school band so that we had a 100-piece band on the field. The bleachers were packed those nights; Tombstone people had never seen such a large band on the football field at home games. I was excited and the students were experiencing tremendous success, very possibly for the first time in their life. Within a short period of time, I was the talk of the town. All our indoor concerts were performed in front of standing room only houses.

One of my greatest successes was with the third and fourth grade recorder class. This simple class soon evolved into a major performing group. I told my superintendent, James "Buck" Clark, that I would love to see the school district invest in different recorders; bass, tenor, and alto recorders added to the soprano recorders would give the class great room for expanding the quality of music to be performed. He told me to go ahead and purchase some of the instruments, staying within the budget of about $200.00, which was a lot of money in 1968.

I made four-part arrangements for the group, and within a relatively short time we were playing some of the classics. One of the elementary classroom teachers was so impressed that she called Dr. Hartsell, chair and professor of music education at the University of Arizona. Dr. Hartsell made a special trip to Tombstone to hear the group and he extended an invitation to perform for future music teachers at the university. This was a great honor for the Tombstone School District; nothing like it had ever happened in that small town. Buck Clark gave authorization for a school bus and for lunches for the forty-plus students and chaperones.

We performed in Crowder Hall at the School of Music

before an almost-full house that included some of the professors. The kids behaved like a bunch of professionals and performed very well without the slightest nervousness. We played four-part Bach, the Humming Chorus from "Madam Butterfly" by Puccini, and some other simpler arrangements. The audience went wild, followed by a standing ovation. We all enjoyed the reception we received; I was very proud of the students, as were the chaperones. After that we had a nice relaxing picnic at Reid Park.

A few weeks later I received a letter from Dr. Hartsell. In it he extended an official invitation for the recording class to perform at the Music Educators National Conference to be held in Honolulu, Hawaii, in the spring of 1969. This was a tremendous honor, but we had to turn it down. There was no way such a large amount of money could have been raised in that small, poor town.

In the spring of my second year in Tombstone I took all my bands to one of the professional recording studios in Tucson. The bands were recorded and an LP was made. (For the younger folks, an LP was a long-playing record; today we have CDs). This was the first of the many recordings I made with my other high school bands. The records sold like hotcakes every time we produced one, preserving a priceless memory for all who participated.

In the meantime Michael was attending kindergarten and Linda was doing some Head Start program work. She kept up with her voice lessons, while I kept commuting to Tucson regularly to play with the Tucson Syphony Orchestra. On rehearsal nights with the symphony, I would leave Tombstone around 4:30 P.M. arriving around 6:00 P.M., giving me plenty of time to have a good warm-up before the start of the rehearsal at 7:00 P.M. In those days the symphony rehearsals lasted three hours, compared to today's two-and-one-half. On rehearsal nights I would get home around midnight and on concert nights close to 1:00 A.M. Each symphony concert gave two performances (Tuesdays and Wednesdays nights); each concert required five rehearsals. Going back and forth between Tombstone and Tucson was tiring, but I was young (thirty years old) and full of energy and enthusiasm. I can proudly state that I never missed either a single rehearsal or a performance with the TSO while commuting; and never missed a day of teaching during my two years of tenure in Tombstone.

I found out that a new high school was opening in the fall of 1969 in Tucson on the far east side called Santa Rita High School. I applied for the position of band director to that newly formed school. Before I turned in my application I approached Buck Clark, superintendent of the Tombstone schools, and told him about my intentions. I also told him that I was willing to stay in Tombstone if I could get a large increase in salary. He told me to go ahead and put in my application and not to waste my talents in the little town any longer. He also told me that I would be missed greatly, but my future was more important.

In a few weeks Hank Slagle, principal of the Santa Rita High School, traveled to Tombstone with two of his assistant principals to observe my teaching. They were in my classroom only for a few minutes. I didn't know what to think. Later that day Buck Clark came to see me, telling me that Hank Slagle had only one major concern: how well do I communicate with my thick accent to my students? Buck Clark assured them that it was not a problem.

In a few weeks I received a contract from Santa Rita High School and was offered the position of director of bands. Both Linda and I were happy for my appointment and so were Michael's grandparents. Having their grandson close by meant a lot to them. They adored Michael. For Linda and me, my new job put an end to the many hours of traveling.

Years later I had a chance to look at my files at the Tucson Unified School District's main office. Most of my files were on microfilm. By pure accident I came across of some of my recommendations from previous professors, principals, etc. Buck Clark's from Tombstone was one of them. His words to the administration of Santa Rita High School made me speechless:

"Dear Mr. Slagle, …this man is a gold mine, don't pass up the opportunity to hire him…" Shortly after I left Tombstone, Buck Clark became superintendent of the Nogales School District. I do see him and his wife Marsha every so often.

Teaching in Tombstone was a great learning experience for me as a starting teacher. I learned more and more as days went by. I invited from the Tucson area more experienced directors than myself, watching them as they worked with my band, learning from their vast experiences. Gordon Solie was one of these people who unselfishly shared his knowledge with me. He was a college band director on sabbatical leave from Portland, Oregon, working on his doctorate at the University of Arizona. I lost contact with him about thirty years ago. Gordon was one of the best in the business.

During the summer of 1969 we packed our belongings into a rented U-Haul and made our move to Tucson into a rented house close to Santa Rita High. There was a huge farewell party given to us by the students and parents. There were many tears shed that night; they all wished us the very best. I think back to my Tombstone years with fond memories and I think Linda and Michael feel the same way as I do, although Michael was too young to make judgments.

13

Santa Rita High School

Band Director at Santa Rita High School

Tucson Unified School District #1 had two new high schools ready to open in the fall of 1969; one on the far west side of town, the other on the far east side. Cholla High School on the west side had already hired a band director earlier in the year. Hank Slagle, the newly appointed principal at Santa Rita High School, wasn't in a hurry to hire his faculty. He was a highly respected man in his position; he was known to hire the best possible faculty member for the job. He hand picked his teaching staff and I felt greatly honored to have been among the chosen ones.

Since Santa Rita High was a brand new school I decided to write a school song and dedicate it to my new school. I spent the summer months working on the fight song and when it was finished I called it the "Golden Eagle March." The school mascot was an eagle and the colors were green and gold. More than thirty years later the same school song is still being played at football games.

Mike was enrolled at Marshall Elementary School while Linda decided that she wanted to concentrate more on her voice. She told me that talking all day long in the classroom wasn't good for someone with aspirations to become a fine singer. She stayed away from classroom teaching for the next fifteen years.

    Santa Rita opened in the fall with 400 students but no seniors. I had forty students signed up for band, over sixty percent of them freshmen. The rest, sophomores and juniors, were transfers from their previous high schools. Having so many freshmen was a blessing; I had a chance to develop their abilities during the next four years. I remember that class very well and thirty-some years later I still see their faces and remember most of the names. The class of 1973 will always be very special to me. This was the band that established my reputation as band director, not just in Tucson but in the state of Arizona as well.

    Because of the low numbers, to have full-time status I had to travel to Duffy Elementary to teach two classes of band and drive to Tucson High to help band director Charles Steele with his top band. Little did I know that I would be retiring and ending my teaching career at Tucson High thirty years later.

    By the third year at Santa Rita I didn't have to travel to other schools anymore as the band had grown in size every year from forty the first year to sixty-four the next year, followed by eighty-eight. During the 1972-1973 school year we marched ninety-six on the football field, plus one drum major and some alternates. After the second year all incoming freshmen were put into the "Freshmen Band." Exceptional freshman had a chance to audition into the top band and if they passed the audition the condition was that they were to be in both bands. No exception was made; the decision was up to those few lucky ones who passed the try-out tests. I don't recall a single person who turned down the offer. By this time the Santa Rita Band had the reputation of being the best-sounding band on the football field and on the concert stage. We were the only marching band that played classical music on the field and were known for it. We received our share of "Superior" ratings at the many different band competitions whether in the marching or concert format.

Santa Rita High School

During the fall of 1972, after marching season I was passing out music for the holiday concert, and music to be performed at TUSD's All-City Band Festival that took place every year in the early part of February. In this festival all TUSD high schools presented their top band, performing in front of parents and other high school bands. Because there were eight high schools (Sabino didn't open until the middle of the 1970s) in the district, the festival was divided into two evenings. It was to be held in the auditorium at Palo Verde High School. I always liked that stage since the Tucson Symphony had used it before moving into the Music Hall in 1971. The schools scheduled to perform were Sahuaro, Santa Rita, Catalina, and host Palo Verde. The remaining schools, Tucson, Rincon, Pueblo, and Cholla, were to perform the following night on the Rincon stage.

As we were preparing for the holiday concert a few students approached me suggesting the band play the "1812 Overture" by Tchaikovsky. I dismissed their recommendation on the grounds that it was too difficult of a piece for us to do. The title "1812" was becoming the buzzword in the band and more and more of the students were bugging me: "…Mr. V, we can do it!" The same day I called Music Land and ordered the band arrangement for the "1812 Overture."

As we were working on holiday music, slowly we took our first steps in trying to master Tchaikovsky's work. The band got excited about the challenge and I had never heard so much individual practicing before or after school in my short teaching career. Huge posters with drawings of cannons were created by the students and were taped to the walls. Every poster had "1812" on it in large numbers. I got excited also, and with the rest of the students couldn't wait for the holiday concert to be over and for school to start again in January after the winter vacation.

The first triumph

January arrived and so did the performance date in February. We were the third band to perform that night and while the first two bands were performing we were seated in the reserve sections listening to the other schools. The students were excited and were waiting with anticipation for their turn. Personally, I couldn't wait to get on stage. I felt good knowing that I had prepared the band the very best I could. Finally it was our turn and the band started to walk out from their seats in a single file carrying their instruments. I turned around towards the audience and noticed that the auditorium was totally full. Some nervousness was taking place in my stomach. I wanted the band to do well more than anything else at that moment.

The curtain was pulled on the stage and we started to set up. Dr. Max Ervin, director of music education at TUSD, was doing his usual job as master of ceremonies at these festivals. He enjoyed talking to the audience, telling jokes, and took great pride showcasing the district's high school music program to them. I liked Max Ervin for he was a fine person and a fine musician. During my early years he told me that one of the best things that ever happened at TUSD was the day when they hired László Veres as band director. Of course I took the compliment seriously; the remark made me feel important for it gave me a boost, knowing that I was doing a good job. Years later at a get-together I overheard Max talking to another band director telling him the same remark that he had told me years earlier. By that time I knew Max better and when I heard his remark I started to laugh at him for being so full of hot air. Nevertheless, at the time he made me feel good as he made many others also. He had a gift for that and I admired him for it.

On stage he noticed my tenseness and tried to calm me down by telling me to take my time with the warm up for there was no hurry. After playing some scales slowly and some final

Santa Rita High School

tuning, I motioned to him that we were ready. I walked off stage and waited for his introduction.

While a student at the university, a special session was offered to us students by Eugene Conley, professor of voice studies, about how to enter the stage for a performance—whether a singer, soloist, accompanist, or conductor. He told us not to look at the audience or wave to them, but go directly to the designated spot and when in place bow to the audience to accept their applause. Bowing simply said "thank you" for welcoming me as a performer to the stage. As the curtain opened I remembered Mr. Conley's words and entered the stage, going directly to the podium. I took my bow front of the audience just as he showed us years ago.

I turned to the band and gave my downbeat to start "1812 Overture." I must have been totally immersed in Tchaikovsky's music, which is about fifteen minutes long. The only thing I was hearing was nothing but sounds and before I realized it I was holding the last note of the overture, ready to give the cutoff signal to the band. Where did the time go, I asked myself. It couldn't be the end; after all we just started to play. But the fact remained; we played everything from beginning to end and we played it to the best of our ability. I gave the final cutoff and a big smile was on my face as I looked at my students. Behind me the audience gave tremendous applause with the yelling of bravos coming from all parts of the auditorium. I motioned to the band to stand up and as I looked at them I saw ninety-seven satisfied faces telling me that we "did it." I turned to the audience to bow and when I finally looked up I noticed the whole auditorium was full of people standing, still applauding. This went on and on until finally Max Ervin motioned for the curtain to be closed. The Santa Rita Band received its first standing ovation, to be followed by many more as the years went by. Max came over and shook my hand. The only thing he said to me was, "I didn't think you could do it." On that Tuesday night in February 1973, the reputation of the Santa Rita Band was established and never faltered during my stay. From that

No Regrets

night on the students always asked me, "Mr. V, what is our big piece for next year?"

One of my biggest goals as a teacher was established: my students were excited about music as I slowly introduced a bunch of rock-and-roll loving teenagers to the love and magic of the classics. Twenty-some years later my ex-students remind me when I run into them: "Mr. V, do you remember when we played 'Capriccio Italien' or 'Universal Judgement' or 'Carmina Burana' or 'Pictures at an Exhibition' or 'Lincoln's Portrait'?" I do remember them well, but most of all I'm glad that those classic pieces of music gave my students a great deal of enjoyment and delight.

Michael attended most of the marching practices on Wednesday nights and football games on Friday nights. He was well liked and all the students in the band knew him. At times a band member would give him a clarinet to carry as he or she was helping him march along the way. He was well liked not because he was Mr. V's son, but because he was Mike Veres, a very fine youngster who was friendly with everybody and had (and still has) a wonderful personality.

During the early years at Santa Rita, Linda told me many times to play a patriotic number like "God Bless America" at one of the concerts. She went on by saying that the audience would love it and they would love me for playing it. I told her that I would have to find an arrangement first and at the same time I tried to ignore her suggestion. She attended the next holiday concert given by my band and as soon I got home she said, "László, you have to play something like 'God Bless America' and if anybody should play anything patriotic it ought to be you, because you came from a communist country." While I wasn't sold on the idea at first, as time went by I began formulating plans, as her suggestion was taking hold of me.

Soon I found myself in the store called Music Land searching for the right type of music. The front cover of one of the pieces of music grabbed my eyes. It showed an old military drum with an old bugle next to it in a color photograph. The title of the music was "Battle Hymn of the Republic." I bought it and started to rehearse it for the 1974 spring concert. I placed it first on the program as an opener. It was received with an incredible ovation. From that day on I played that composition as the band's final number, except for one concert. I was under the impression that the audience got tired of it and it was time to table it for a while. How wrong I was. Parents were telling me how much they were looking forward to every concert given by the Santa Rita Band under László Veres' direction, and how much they were looking forward to hearing "The Battle Hymn" at the concert. From that day on, every one of my high school band performances ended with that marvelous patriotic arrangement by James Ployhar. Linda had the right vision, and was absolutely correct in her prediction. I thanked Linda for bugging me, and not letting up on her suggestion.

Death of my father

Sunday, July 3, 1977, started out to be a fine day. Like many other Americans during the Fourth of July weekend, we were having our family barbecue in the backyard. In the middle of the afternoon the phone rang and it was my brother Zoli on the other end. From his voice I could tell that something was very wrong. With great difficulty and with a crying voice he told me that our beloved father had just died a few minutes before in an accident.

Father was a heavy smoker and the doctor told him that he must stop. He kept on smoking behind our mother's back. According to Zoli, father in his later years tried to get away from everybody to light up a cigarette. On this Sunday afternoon my brother Pista was having a family gathering at his home in Burbank. Father was outside teaching his grandson Robby how to ride a bike and at one point decided to get on the bike for a demonstration and to have a smoke down the block. The street was slightly angled and as he was going downhill with increased speed he lost control of the bike and at the intersection a pickup truck hit him. It was instant death. It was a very sad moment and was a major blow to all of us children, but especially to mother. Suddenly she had lost her partner after more than forty-five years of marriage. While in his mind he was still a young man, in reality he was a very sick man with serious heart, lung, and arthritis problems. He was to be 72 years old at the end of July. I think of him often. I imagine that he would be proud of my achievements. I know my mother is.

Along with my full-time job as band director I kept up my playing with the Tucson Symphony as principal clarinetist. I had the great fortune and privilege of playing many of the greatest musical masterpieces created by human beings. I also had private students on the side.

Because of my busy schedule the time was racing by. I didn't have much of a family life and the marriage between Linda and me was slowly disintegrating, ending eventually in divorce several years later, after almost twenty-two years of marriage. At the time of the marriage dissolution, Mike was twenty-one years old, not a child anymore. Most likely the breakup of the marriage was my fault. I still keep in touch with Linda and we enjoy visiting on the phone once or twice a year. I always ask Michael how his mother is doing.

14

Picking up the Baton

Getting involved with orchestral conducting

In the spring of 1975, maestro Gregory Millar, conductor of the Tucson Symphony Orchestra, approached me and asked if I would have any interest in taking over the Tucson Symphony Youth Orchestra as conductor. I told him that I had absolutely no knowledge of the string instruments that make up the bulk of the orchestra. His reply was that I shouldn't worry about that part for he would supply a string coach. I told him I wasn't really interested, however I would think about it.

A day later I received a phone call from Ed Murphy, music professor at the university and a parent who had a son in the youth orchestra. He told me that I should give serious consideration to the offer that was made to me. He continued by saying that I had the reputation as a highly energetic person on the podium with a special gift to excite young musicians and to pull music out of them. He went on and talked about my great success with the Santa Rita Band and used it as an example. I thanked him for his confidence in me and truly appreciated his call. After talking it over with Linda, I called the symphony office to accept their offer for a year, to give it a try.

My schedule was full. I was a full-time teacher, principal clarinetist in the symphony, private teacher, and now an added responsibility. Hard work never bothered me; the added task didn't scare me at all. I guess ego played a great deal in my decision. What was to happen to my family life? The truth was, that by this time, sorry to say, Linda and I were on totally different wave lengths and divorce was just a few years away. Only Michael kept me in that house.

I remember the program I picked for the first youth orchestra concert: Kabalevsky's "Colas Breugnon" Overture; Schubert's "Unfinished Symphony," and the "Pines of Rome" by Respighi. This was a very ambitious program and a challenge for everyone involved.

The concert date arrived and it was a success. The parents were impressed and the musicians excited. Maestro Millar was impressed also. The spring concert was just as successful and the parents and musicians were eagerly looking forward to the next season with me as their leader.

By this time I was excited about my new responsibility. The youth orchestra was made up of the finest high school musicians in the metropolitan Tucson area and was performing at a higher level than the Santa Rita Band was capable of. I also loved the warm, luxuriant sounds of the strings. Because of my love affair with the orchestra's sound I always approached and conducted the band as an orchestra also. For this I was criticized by many of the "band purists" and it holds through even today. Many reminded me that the concert band is a totally different ensemble from the orchestra and should be approached as such. To me music was music, and personally I love to hear the full sonorous sounds, whether orchestra or concert band.

Picking up the Baton

Birth of the Philharmonia Orchestra of Tucson

At the end of the season with the youth orchestra, the Tucson Symphony board notified me that my services were no longer needed and Mr. Paul Walker would take over the conducting duties of the orchestra. When the parents and students found out about it, they were up in arms and went to the board with their complaints, expressing their frustrations. The board stood with their decision and parents' complaints were ignored. These parents approached me and wanted to know if I would be interested in being a conductor of a newly formed orchestra. They were willing to put in the effort to form a new organization away from the Tucson Symphony. I felt honored and told them to go ahead with the plans.

We worked very hard on the new project and by September we had an orchestra of about sixty or seventy players ready to start rehearsals at the Temple of Music and Art on Scott Avenue downtown. We borrowed music from local high school orchestra directors who were supporting us. I suggested the name Philharmonia Orchestra of Tucson for the newly formed group, and this was accepted by the supporters. In the fall of 1976 the Philharmonia was born while after a so-so season the Tucson Symphony Youth Orchestra folded in the spring of 1977, for lack of interest from both the young musicians and parents.

Debut performance of the Philharmonia Orchestra of Tucson, 1977

No Regrets

    The Tucson Symphony board was in a difficult situation. The orchestra members elected me to be their representative on the board and while I was sitting in on board meetings, they had to discuss the youth orchestra problems in front of me. While I had a good time, the board president was furious with me. My presence at these meetings was embarrassing for all who were responsible for getting me out as conductor of the youth group. At one of the meetings the president announced to the board members in my presence that the youth orchestra was folding. A vote was taken and not a single person voted to keep the youth orchestra alive under the symphony's umbrella. I was called a revolutionary by the board president, who put all the blame on me. Twenty-six years later the Philharmonia is still alive and doing well. At times I run into Paul Skinner, president of the symphony board at that time, and he is trying very hard to be on friendly terms with me.

    I led the Philharmonia orchestra successfully for seven years, premiering new works along the way that got the attention of the media and the public. The orchestra featured fine artists from the university faculty as soloists and also talented musicians as soloists from the orchestra (I have always been a great advocate of introducing fine young talents to the public). We were receiving good coverage from both of the local papers and from TV stations as well. We made a recording titled "Cello Time in Tucson" with Professor Gordon Epperson as cello soloist and the record was released nationwide, for sale. KUAT television station made a professional video of one of our performances and that was released nationally also.

    In 1983 I requested a leave of absence from the Tucson School District (TUSD), Tucson Symphony, and the Philharmonia for a year. Only TUSD granted me the leave, while the other two organizations declined it. I ended my association with the Tucson Symphony after sixteen years as principal clarinetist and my association with the Tucson Philharmonia after being its founder and its first music director/conductor for seven years. For both of

Picking up the Baton

the latter organizations I always gave my very best, performing steadily at a high professional level, never missing rehearsals or performances along the way and never being late for any of the activities even while commuting from Tombstone. These organizations expected loyalty from their employees; however, when it was time for them to show appreciation to their performers the gratitude became non-existent. Such is life! I was saddened at first, but got over it very quickly. The irony is that I have guest-conducted the Tucson Symphony Orchestra numerous times in the last ten-plus years.

In 1980 I was asked to take over the orchestra called "Orchestai," a semi-professional orchestra made up of professional musicians with not much pay. That is why I call it semi-professional. The name of the orchestra was changed to Arizona Touring Orchestra and I did the conducting duties successfully until it folded in 1984 for lack of financial support. The ATO was a very fine chamber-size orchestra, and I truly enjoyed working with them.

In 1980 I was also asked to conduct the Simon Peter Orchestra and led that group until I resigned eighteen years later. The Simon Peter production became an annual event in Tucson attended by thousands of people during the Easter season. The orchestra members were paid, but not enough to attract the fine musicians from the Tucson Symphony. Although I tried very hard, the orchestra was average at best, but still good enough for the production.

During all this time I was the band director at Santa Rita until 1983. I decided to take a leave of absence. I was going through a divorce and the best thing for me was to get out of town and to get away from all the hectic workload I was carrying. My brother Zoli offered me a job in his import-export business in Los Angeles, a job I kept, until I decided to move back to Tucson to continue my teaching career in 1985.

While in L.A. I attended many concerts given by the Los Angeles Philharmonic, and musicals and theater productions. I took some business classes at UCLA and visited many places including the famous Crystal Cathedral in Anaheim.

    I spent a great amount of time with my mother and we visited the Hungarian Tokay restaurant every Wednesday for the early-bird special that ended at 5:30 P.M. When we were a few minutes late mother would remind everybody, "We are here, we are here, and the time is 5:30 sharp." She went by her watch and not by the restaurant's clock on the wall. She didn't want us to be charged with evening meal prices. They knew us well and the owner and his staff got a good chuckle out of mother's remarks. I always looked forward to dinners with her and had many fine conversations between the two of us. I treasure those pleasant, enjoyable times with her.

    Mother was never known to be a shy person. One day I told her that I wanted to buy myself a gold necklace for my pendant "chai." She was insisting to go shopping with me. I remember well going into a privately owned jewelry store with her. The necklace was beautiful and I liked it a lot. It was heavy and I figured the price would be high and it was. After the owner quoted the price I thought it sounded right after doing much window-shopping myself. Mother's reaction was different, and she said something like, "If I wanted to hear jokes I would have gone to a theater that offers comedy." She went on, "Now tell me the real price," and made an offer that was less than half of the asking price. I was embarrassed and was ready to leave the store. After bargaining back and forth in the end I paid a little over half of the original asking price for the necklace.

    In postwar Europe bartering was the only way to do business, since the paper money was worthless, and as far as bargaining goes, it was always expected in dealing with goods. To her, bargaining was the natural way to do business. That is our mother!

Picking up the Baton

Some interesting and amusing events at Santa Rita

My first year at Santa Rita was challenging. I had forty students in the band, most of them freshmen. The others were sophomores and juniors who came from different high schools. Since we were a brand new school, there was no senior class. The typical student comment was, "At the previous school we did it this way," etc. My quick response was, "Do I look like your other teacher; do I speak like your previous teacher? My name is Mr. Veres and this is Santa Rita High School and we will do things my way." There were no more like comments after that. They were testing me for sure, but didn't take long for them to find out who was running the show and who was in control.

We were rehearsing this certain musical number and I was after one of the saxophone players, asking him to play a passage over and over again. He was a junior and his name was Roger. The passage wasn't difficult at all but he was having a hard time with it. The reason I kept nagging was because he was the main instigator who started the "my other band directors did it this way and that way" comments. Finally he couldn't take my nagging anymore and with anger on his face he stood up, came to my podium, handed me his saxophone, and said, "…OK, wise guy, you do it!" I asked him jokingly, "Would you like to put a dollar on it?" He replied, "Let's make it five." There was total silence in the band; a pin drop could have been heard. I took his instrument, cleaned the mouthpiece, and played the passage perfectly. He grabbed his instrument and like a dog with its tail between its legs walked back to his seat. The rest of the rehearsal and subsequent rehearsals went very nicely. The bell rang and the class emptied. I was preparing to go to my next class when the door opened and in walked Roger. Without saying a word he put a $5.00 bill on the table and left. No student ever challenged me in the following thirty years of teaching.

Rick Matthews, the band's lead trumpet player, had surgery

No Regrets

done on his toe on a Friday, the day of a football game and the marching band's performance. To my surprise he showed up that evening barely able to walk, with a huge bandage on his foot. When I questioned him about his presence he answered back, "Mr. Veres, I just couldn't let the band down." Without shoes he marched the entire show, limping during the whole time. That is either dedication or being crazy. Needless to say, I was touched and used his devotion as an example to future students many times.

In my early teaching years I quickly learned not to judge a book by its cover. A young incoming freshman showed up in the spring to audition for the top band. She was heavy-set and was carrying a snare drum under her arm. I was telling myself, "Oh God, another drummer and besides, no band uniform would fit her." She proceeded to set up her snare drum and I asked her to demonstrate certain rudiments, (rolls etc.) on her instrument. She did everything I asked for very well. Finally I said to her, "Can you read?" Her answer was a confident "yes." I put something on the difficult side in front of her to sight-read, thinking that it would get to her. Without any hesitation she played the whole piece without mistakes. I had met Tracy Sullivan! As time went by she developed into one of the finest high school musicians I have ever known, culminating as top percussionist in the state of Arizona by her senior year. We had to have a special uniform made for her. I never found out until after graduation that she was on strict doctor's orders not to participate in any physical education classes. That included marching band, due to her very small heart. Although she had many other ailments, Tracy never missed a single marching band performance. Her positive attitude and constant smile was contagious and her personality lit up the room any time she walked in. She loved band and she loved music. Twenty-plus years later I still keep in touch with her. I can honestly state that throughout the years I had many Tracys and Ricks in my bands.

I had a national wrestling champion in the band for three years. His name was Bill Rosado and he played the flute. He was

Picking up the Baton

short, weighed fewer than 100 pounds, with solid muscles. He made the U.S. Olympic wrestling team in his senior year in high school. Bill was undefeated in meets during his junior and senior years. I saw him in competition only once. He was lightning fast, strong, and all his opponents were pinned in a relatively short time. There were a few times when Bill was late to class and times like that I wasn't too nice to the late comers. On one occasion I had to leave the classroom for a minute and I noticed Bill sitting on the floor with his books. I questioned what he was doing and his reply made me laugh. He told me that he was late and was scared to walk in for I would yell at him. Bill also told me that there were only two people he was afraid of: his mother and Mr. Veres.

One day there were about ten guys in the band room during lunch when Bill walked in. Bill wasn't ready to defend himself when five big boys grabbed him from his blind side to get him on the floor for a good "pinky." Pulling up one's shirt to expose the bare stomach was the first step to a pinky. With the palm of the hand the stomach would be hit repeatedly until the flesh turned to a pink color. That was to be done to Bill. I walked in just as they were trying to get Bill down. His quickness was very impressive; the big boys couldn't bring him down. I finally stepped in to stop the fooling around. Bill's face was red and sweaty and the other boys were sitting on the floor totally exhausted, breathing heavily. Bill looked at me innocently and said, "Mr. Veres, I came in to find out my semester grade and this is what happened." I discovered later that the boys who jumped Bill were on the wrestling team also and were good friends. All five of them couldn't take him down although they were in higher weight divisions. We all had a good laugh.

The students and parents affectionately started to call me "Mr. V" by my third year, and later on the students would call me "King V." I'm not sure if I want to know what they called me behind my back.

The following story was related to me. A certain not-so-

No Regrets

good trumpet player by the name of Norton was one of the biggest goof-offs in school. I yelled and screamed at him numerous times to shape up. Finally I kicked him out of the band and the counselor removed him from my class. A year or so later a bunch of students gathered in front of a Circle K store across the street from the school. A certain student who wasn't in band was calling me dirty names in front of Norton and others. Norton went up to this person, punched him in the mouth, and told him, "The man's name is "King V" and don't you ever forget it." I couldn't believe my ears; this person whom I had kicked out of the band was defending me in front of others. This incident made me feel good.

Connie was a bassoon player in the band. She was extremely well built; all the right curves were in the right places. In the marching band she would play the clarinet, for I would not allow the bassoon on the football field for marching due to the high price of the instrument. She asked me if she could play the cymbals. I said, "No, Connie; we have enough cymbal players already and besides all the cymbals are being used." She wouldn't take no for an answer; on the other hand, I wasn't about to give in to her.

A few weeks later all my cymbal players were absent one day and I called Connie in my office. I asked her if she was still interested in playing the cymbals. She was in heaven and had an ear-to-ear smile. I gave her the biggest and heaviest cymbals we had with the hope that it would discourage her from playing that instrument in the future. She was a good bassoonist and clarinet player and that is where I needed her.

She was happy and joined the percussion section on the field. The band was spread out on the field as individual sections were practicing their assignments until we put the whole band together. At one point I heard a huge scream coming from one end of the field. I didn't pay much attention since the school was surrounded by desert and one would regularly see scorpions, snakes, and other bugs that would scare people, especially girls. After rehearsal Connie walked into my office and said, "Mr. Veres, I'm

Picking up the Baton

black and blue all over." I was expecting to see marks on her hand and wrist from carrying the cymbals. I said, "Let me see it," and she said, "I'm not going to show it to you." I said okay and went to teach my next class. Later on I found out that the scream came from Connie, for while smashing the cymbals she accidentally pinched her nipple. Connie never asked to play cymbals again: her cymbal playing career ended in less than forty-five minutes.

Brand new uniforms came in big cardboard boxes. After we removed the uniforms, the empty boxes were stacked for the custodian to take out after school. I was teaching a class when one of the students told me that one of the boxes was moving back and forth in the hallway and I should see it. Sure enough, the box was moving fast and was moving away from me. At the end of the hallway it made a U-turn and was moving toward me at a relatively high speed. I put my foot up and the box came to a sudden halt due to the impact. The box stood up and out came Steve, totally glazed, not realizing what had happened. Finally he spoke, "Oh, it's you; I thought I hit the wall." It took some time before Steve's head stopped spinning.

Charlie, one of the band's baritone players, showed up to the band room one day with a stock he made at home as a project for one of his classes. These stocks were used in colonial times especially in Massachusetts, in public places. People who broke the law were put there for all to see. After he did his presentation he asked me if he could keep it in the band room until his ride showed up in a day or two. I told him it was no problem and it was placed front of the blackboard. The next morning a message was on the blackboard, "If you mess around in band, you will end up in it."

We had a drummer who liked to mess around a lot and was making bragging remarks like, "Nobody will put me into that thing." During lunch I went to the administration building to get my mail. On the way back, as soon as I entered the hallway, I heard some incredible screaming coming from the band room. I started

No Regrets

to run, opened the closed band room door and saw Greg Valdez, the drummer, in the stock. He was totally helpless; he could not move. One of the boys was tickling his nose with a feather; one of them was giving him the pinky, and one of them was pulling out his chest hair one by one. He was being tortured. I yelled at the top of my lungs, "Get him out of there," and told Charlie to take his stock home right away. Just for the record, Greg became a sweet person and never messed around after that incident.

Brenda, a trumpet player, was the band president in her senior year. She was a nice quiet person with a good sense of humor. Boys liked to pick on her. I kept the band room open during lunches because students liked to hang around. To me the band room was a home away from home, a place for my students.

During one lunch period three or four boys got hold of Brenda and were in the process of stuffing her in one of the larger instrument lockers. Once again I was hearing screaming and laughter coming out of the band room as I was returning from the administration building. The boys were on their knees shoving Brenda into the locker that was located on the bottom. The only thing I saw were three butts sticking out, all of them belonging to the boys. I grabbed my plastic conducting baton and held the fat part of it in my right hand; pulled back the tip with my left hand flexing it like a bow ready to be shot. In rapid motion I got all the butts in a hurry. The boys tried to jump up, but since they were on top of each other the person on the bottom released the biggest yell. While the boys on the top could grab their butts and scratch, Bill, one of the horn players, was totally helpless. I was yelling at them, "Get up and let her out of the locker!" Finally they untangled and stood up, massaging their rear ends. Brenda thanked me. Her hair was a mess and her clothes pulled in all directions. All the bystanders had a good chuckle, including me. The baton hurts on a rear end, and for me, that was the quickest way to break up that incident.

While at Santa Rita, Gary Stephan and Roger Shanley, two

Picking up the Baton

faculty members at the school, introduced me to long-distance running as a form of exercise. I was slightly overweight at the time and needed some physical activity to shed some pounds. Roger ran the Boston Marathon every year and started to talk to me about running a marathon one day. I began to enter races sponsored by the local Road Runners Club, just for the fun of it. Before I knew it, I was running regularly 5K and 10K races, finishing each race in the middle of the pack. One day I ran sixteen miles in practice, the most I ever did at any one time. I told myself that if I could do sixteen miles, then I should be able to do twenty-six miles, the distance for the marathon.

In 1981, at the age of forty-four I decided to enter the Tucson Marathon. I finished the twenty-six miles and 365 yards in four hours and forty minutes and I wasn't the last person across the finish line; I passed many people the last four or five miles. That

The final yards of the Tucson Marathon, 1981

was something I had always wanted to do for myself and I was very proud of my accomplishment. I also have to admit that I had a difficult time walking for a whole week, due to muscle soreness.

During the summer of 1972 I went back to Eugene, Oregon, to finish my master's degree program. I was one class short of the requirements and also had to finish a research paper for the "Music in the Renaissance" class that I had taken five years earlier. At the end of the summer session I was the proud recipient of the Master of Music degree from the University of Oregon. On the way home from Eugene I stopped in Los Angeles to visit my parents, my brother Zoli, and his family. The rest of the three brothers were living in Boston that time. My parents and Zoli were so proud of my achievement that they surprised me with a brand new Buffet "A" clarinet as a graduation gift. I played that instrument in the symphony orchestra for many years and I still play on it today. It is a very fine instrument and one day I shall pass it on to my son Daniel.

My bike accident

As a band we would do many things together outside the band room, for socializing. The annual yearbook signing party took place at our backyard on 29th Street many times, or we rented the pool facility at Rolling Hills subdivision. Times like this I was the chef, cooking burgers and hotdogs on the grill. I always had a good time doing it. Many times just before the start of the new school year we would take hikes, inviting all incoming freshmen to welcome them into our band, which was my extended family. Some of the hikes included Seven Falls in Sabino Canyon, or picnic areas at Sahuaro National Monument East.

In early May 1976 we gathered in front of our house to take a bike ride to the monument. Many students showed up and we headed to the recently built and freshly oiled bike path on Old Spanish Trail. It was a beautiful Saturday morning in Tucson and

Picking up the Baton

it was refreshing to be outdoors.

Most of the students were fast bikers and quickly disappeared in the distance. Midway out on the trail going uphill, I stood up on the pedals to make the pedaling less strenuous. Suddenly the front wheel hit a small piece of rock and slipped under me. I flew across the handlebars landing full force on my elbow and my chin. In the very last second I managed to protect my face with my left arm, which turned out to be a blessing. Some blood was dripping on my shirt, however. At the time I didn't feel any pain nor did I realize the damage that was done to my face.

After a few minutes I got on the bike and started to pedal again. This time the blood was dripping down on my shirt faster and faster. I got off the bike to slow down my heartbeat and with unhurried steps began to push the bike towards the monument. At the picnic area the students looked me and their facial expression said it all. I must have looked like a mess. They called Linda for me who drove out to pick me up. When she saw me she just said, "Oh my God."

At home I had a chance to look at myself in the mirror. My face was slowly becoming the size of a basketball, my front teeth were pushed up to my nose, my lower lip had a small opening where the lower teeth cut through, while the upper lip was as large as a hotdog.

First thing Monday morning I went to see my dentist who told me that nothing could be done until the swelling disappeared. A few weeks later I had major surgery done: four of my front teeth had to be removed and a bridge had to be built. I was questioning my future as a clarinet player. Would I ever be able to play again?

By the end of July I received my bridge and started to practice ever so slowly while going through some drastic embouchure changes. With excruciating pain I began to play "double lip" and was seeing stars from the pain caused by the upper lip's tenderness. Gradually I was relearning how to play my instrument by using no pressure on my teeth. The diligent, patient practice did

No Regrets

pay off; by September I was performing again as the symphony's principal clarinet player, a position I held until my retirement in 1983. More than twenty-five years later I still play my clarinet, but not professionally. I play it well enough to perform a solo with the Arizona Symphonic Winds on occasion, and to teach my son Daniel the art of clarinet playing. I do sporadically play duets with him and André.

    Recently, my bridge had to be replaced for the first time.

15

Mary McGrath

Mary McGrath, mother of André and Daniel

By the middle of the 1980s, Mary McGrath and I were dating. She was much younger than I, more mature than her age would indicate. She was well read, and had a good head on her shoulders. She was a clarinet player and after much nagging I took her as a student. It took some convincing that she should finish her degree at the university and not lose all the credits she had accumulated at Concordia College in Fargo-Moorhead, Minnesota. She finally finished the few subjects she needed and with her senior recital the requirements for the bachelor's degree was completed.

When I went to Los Angeles we kept in touch through correspondence and phone calls. I was well aware of the age difference. However, I enjoyed her company. Both of us decided that she should move out to L.A. to be close to each other. This she did and we stayed together in that city until it was time to move back to Tucson in 1985. My leave of absence from the Tucson Unified School District was good only for two years without the penalty of losing my seniority on the pay scale. While in L.A. Mary kept her apartment in Tucson and when we moved back we stayed there.

I had unfinished business in L.A. and had to go back for a few weeks during the summer of 1986. I told Mary to look for housing in the foothills or close to it; however, there was to be a limit on the price. Sure enough, one day I received a phone call from her telling me that she found this house for sale and I should see it right away before it was listed on the market. I took the first flight out of Los Angeles to check the place out. We both liked the house and the decision was made to purchase it. I liked the neighborhood, the location, and the price was right. The owners were still living in the house and our moving in could not happen until October.

By this time I felt a special bond between the two of us and wanted to marry her. I was forty-nine years old at the time and she was twenty-seven. I wanted to have more children even though we knew that because of my advanced age I would not be able to keep up with my children while playing games with them like baseball or other sports activities during their growing years. I was also aware of the fact that by the time I would be in my late sixties my wife would be in her prime years. She would want to get more out of life than to just sit at home with her elderly husband. In no way did I want to be a burden to someone, for I have always been a person who took care of himself, never depending upon anyone. Although I had a full scholarship and part-time jobs while as a student at the university, I felt that I was a burden to Linda during my under- graduate years. I didn't like that at all. For me, supporting my family financially while taking care of myself was a natural thing to do.

While part of me told me not marry someone who was much younger, the other part of me had a greater influence on my decision. I was a dreamer who thought it would work. I loved her and I was happy to be with her and I truly believed it was mutual. For us to get married was the right thing to do and that is how I felt

Mary McGrath

about it. We did many things together and enjoyed each other's company; we had a mutual love for music, hiking, biking, and going to places. In the fall of 1986, after moving into the house, I proposed to her. We were married soon after. Most of her family and all of mine showed up for the wedding, which took place in the Arizona Inn. It was a beautiful occasion and I was very happy.

In the latter part August of 1988 I had a heart attack. I was playing with André on the floor, having the greatest of times. He was giggling non-stop, enjoying his time with me. Suddenly I felt a tremendous weight on my chest and my left arm was going numb. I got on my feet in a hurry and ran out to the backyard where I started to do jumping jacks to get some blood circulation going. I was also doing circular motions with my left arm while telling myself "…this son-of-a-bitch is not going to kill me!" I stayed outside until I felt better. I didn't want Mary to worry about what was going on. I complained to her about a slight chest pain before we went to bed. I took some medication thinking that I was catching cold. Next morning she made me go to the clinic for a checkup, where they hooked me up to the EKG machine. My heartbeat was irregular and I was rushed to the hospital right away. A few days later a triple bypass was performed. The doctors told me that I had had a major heart attack and was lucky to be alive. The recovery took some time. Presently I'm in my fifteenth year with my bypass.

The surgery scared me. What about my family? Who would take care of my young wife with a year-old child? I started to save money diligently, to provide for them in case of some serious emergency. We wanted another child but I was scared, with good reason. Finally the decision was made and in the later part of 1988 Mary became pregnant. Daniel was born the following year.

After the birth of Daniel we slowly started to drift apart. Both of us are hardheaded people and this led to some disagreements among us. She wasn't a person who liked to lose arguments. After awhile I started to ignore her point of view, especially when she was dead wrong, and I would just walk away. Even her mother

No Regrets

used to tell her, "Mary, don't try to win all arguments." We have a saying in Hungarian for someone like that: "túl okos," meaning, "know it all," even when they are wrong.

At Tucson Unified School District she became interested in computers and she dived in with full dedication to learn about them as much as she could. She was an extremely hard worker and in this area she was very intelligent. She devoted her time and energy to learning by attending night school and studying diligently. I told her many times that she would be running the computer department before long and my prediction did come through. Her total dedication to the computers and her work slowly destroyed our marriage and family life. There were times when she would leave the house before the children would be up and not be home until late at night. I would get them up in the morning, wash them, feed them, take them to the babysitter, pick them up, feed them and finally put them to bed. There were many times when only André, Daniel, and myself ate supper while their mother was who knows where. I remember Daniel telling her once, "Why can't you be home with us?" As I see it, she was married to her work instead of me or to the family she always wanted.

The marriage was falling apart and I put the blame on myself for letting it happen. She remarked many times that I didn't support her in her endeavors. The fact is that I did support her and encouraged her to take typing classes; to take the position Tucson Unified District offered to her in the main office; to go to school to learn about computers; and bought a computer to be used at home for practice. At one point she was the principal's secretary at Catalina High School, where she worked very hard. The computer position opened up at the school district's main office and it took some talking on my part to point out to her that the move would be more beneficial for her as far as advancement was concerned, and a lot more challenging. She felt loyalty to the school and to her principal. That was a very grand gesture on her part, but I also told her that her future was more important than her loyalty. The rest is history.

As much as I tried saving the marriage for the sake of the children, it ended after almost twelve years. I take my share of the responsibility for the divorce.

With André, left, Daniel, and mother Mary

André Veres

André was born on a Friday, August 28, 1987 in Tucson. He was delivered with the help of a midwife, as was Daniel two years later. I was present at both of the boys' births; it was exciting to watch the miracle that was taking place. I cut the umbilical cord for both of the boys. When the midwife placed the newborn baby on Mary's bare chest, she started to cry and said, "I don't know what to do: I never had a baby before." I replied, "You learn, and by the way, we have an André." Until that point she didn't even ask if the baby was a boy or a girl. I always liked the name André because of André Previn, the famous conductor-composer-pianist. I loved André from the day he was born. After the midwife cleaned

No Regrets

him up I held him for a long time, showering him with kisses. I always felt that there was a special bond between the two of us, a bond that holds true even today fifteen years later. During the early years I told Mary many times, "I can't picture life B.A." She would look at me like I was some kind of a crazy person until I explained that B.A. stood for "Before André." André was a joy in my life. I would roll on the floor with him; play with him even when he emptied his stomach on me; fed him; and soon changed his diaper. I always believed that André was "Daddy's boy." My love for him is endless even now in his teenage years. I tell him many times, "I'm your Daddy and don't you ever forget it! This Daddy loves you to death!" Actually I do tell the same to Daniel also. I also remind them that they will talk to me with respect and I expect them to do the same with their mother, stepmother, and everybody else for that matter.

I used to pick André up from pre-school on the way home from Tucson High. As soon as he saw me, he would run to me with a big smile saying, "Daddy, Daddy." I would hug him and shower him with kisses. Some of the few clean Hungarian words he learned were "ölelés" (hug) and "kicsi puszikát" (little kisses—I pronounced it "pooffycat").

André was a member of the Tucson Arizona Boys Chorus for five years, where he learned a great deal about music, singing, and performing. He traveled a lot with the chorus that included tours to the Orient, South America, Canada, the Midwest, and Northwest states in the United States, plus Hawaii. He graduated from the chorus in the summer of 2002. He is fifteen years old and a freshman in high school, where plays the trumpet in the band and plays football. In the field of music I find him to be talented. He has been taking private lessons on the instrument for the last two years and it will be interesting to see how far will he go with his trumpet playing and his talent. He won the first trumpet chair position in his high school band as a freshman, beating out upper classmen in the process. I'm very proud of his achievements.

I still give and get my kisses every time I see him. When I talk about the boys or when I see them, I melt. Fran calls me a "marshmallow Daddy."

Duet with André, 2001

Daniel Veres

Daniel was born two years after André on a Monday, September 25, 1989, also in Tucson. Both Mary and I agreed that we should have another child, however, I was frightened of the thought that Mary might become a widow with two young children. My open-heart surgery in 1988 and my advanced age terrified me. Mary wasn't scared. She was a believer that André should have a playmate. I agreed with her, especially since both of us came from large families. Nevertheless, my age was a reality. Now that Daniel is thirteen years old, I am grateful that we have him. I love him dearly, just like André. All of the boys are joys in my life.

From the day Daniel was born he became "mommy's boy." Mary did see the bond between André and me; she wanted to create the same bond with our newborn son. To this day Daniel has always been close to his mother and I'm glad to see that. Actually both boys are very close to both of us. My love for them is most sincere, passionate, and affectionate. When I see them my eyes light up and I'm in heaven.

A few months before Daniel was born, Mary, on one of her many visits to her doctor, had a sonogram done. The doctor was pointing to the picture on the screen highlighting certain parts of that little human being. The heartbeat was visible to me but all other parts were a big blur. At one point he stopped and was pointing to a spot and asked us, "Would you like to know the sex of the baby now or wait until the baby is born?" Mary and I had talked about this before. Knowing the sex ahead of time made it easier for others at the baby shower and for us in the planning. Deep down both of us were hoping for a boy for simple reasons like sharing rooms, and hand-me-downs. I told the doctor, "Yes, we want to know." He was pointing to a blurry part of the picture and said, "There is the plumbing." I was looking for the "plumbing," but the only thing I saw was a big distorted image on the screen and I was asking, "Where, where?" I never did see the plumbing until he was born. He didn't waste time explaining and just continued his examination. As far as coming up with a name, we didn't decide on it until a few hours before birth. I liked the name Daniel, but I was afraid that it might become "Danny." Mary felt the same way and the decision was made that we would insist on calling him Daniel all the time. Of course I have plenty of nicknames for the boys.

I call both of them "papu" (no meaning); "papuka" or "papuci" (both are diminutive forms). If there is a meaning to these nicknames, the meaning is "my passionate love for them." I also call them by using Hungarian words my parents used and my mother at the age of ninety still uses on all of her boys. They are "életem" —my life; "csillagom"—my heavenly star; "édes fiam"—my sweet, darling son. Every time I see them in the morning or after school my greeting is always the same: "Szerbusz (Hi) Papuka," and they reply "Szerbusz Daddy." I give and get my kisses and I'm in ecstasy. I wouldn't trade places with anybody in this world.

In the mornings as they awakened I would massage their backs when they were babies and kiss them to death in the process. This practice still takes place even today. When they feel my hands, they automatically turn on their stomach waiting for their massages.

All massages end with a small whack on their bottom and I tell them that that is the way my daddy used to do it and at the same time he would say, "Time to get up: half a day is already gone." The time was 6:00 AM. I remind both of my boys to make sure they do the same to their children when they become parents, but most of all, make sure they love them.

Daniel, like André, was a member of the Tucson Arizona Boys Chorus and did well. He spent four and one-half years with the organization. He is thirteen years old now and in seventh grade. He plays the clarinet in the band and presently holds the first chair

Duet with Daniel, 2001

clarinet position. Like André, he also has great potential in the field of music. His clarinet playing is improving steadily and for his age he plays well. Recently he received a "Superior" rating for his solo performance at a competition, with his stepmother Fran providing the piano accompaniment. He takes instructions on his instrument from his daddy who doesn't charge much for the tutoring. During lessons Daddy receives many kisses and those kisses are priceless. I'm very proud of Daniel's achievements.

Both boys play in the Foothills Phil Orchestra under my

direction. I'm happy to have them in that group; they are gaining invaluable musical and playing experiences.

Before a Foothills Phil concert—left to right, André, Frances, László, and Daniel

16

Arizona Symphonic Winds

Arizona Symphonic Winds

After returning to Tucson, Mary told me that she would like to play her clarinet again in a group. I told her that there were two community orchestras in town. A concert band that met every Thursday night at one of the local music stores was always looking for clarinet players, especially good ones. At her prime, Mary was a fairly accomplished player and she would have been welcomed with open arms. However, that is not what she had in mind. She wanted to play her clarinet in a group that I was conducting.

I always had a strong desire to form a community concert band and conduct it. Since I had many contacts and knew many musicians, a letter of invitation was sent out, informing them of a newly formed concert band for the sole purpose to read good quality band literature just for the fun of it, under my direction. The response was incredible, with numerous quality players showing interest.

The first rehearsal took place during the first week of February 1986. After a few rehearsals at the Palo Verde High School band room, where I was the band director at the time, one of the tuba players put his hand up and with a deep voice expressed his feeling, "This band sounds great; let's give a concert." The rest of the band members were just as enthused about the idea.

In early May 1986 we made our debut performance at the high school auditorium with great success. Before the performance we had to have a name and since we rehearsed on Monday nights the name "Monday Night Band" was suggested as a joke after "Monday Night Football" on TV. We decided on the name Tucson Symphonic Band and with that performance the newly formed band was born. I'm happy to report that sixteen years later it is still going strong, one of the most respected community musical groups not just in the city of Tucson, but in the whole state. When I transferred to Tucson High School in the fall of 1987, the name Tucson Symphonic Band had to be changed to avoid confusion between the high school band where I was teaching and the community band. Arizona Symphonic Winds became our new name.

The band was rehearsing and giving a few concerts here and there. The recently built Udall Park on the city's far east side was ready to be dedicated, and on Mary's suggestion we volunteered the Symphonic Winds to perform at the dedication ceremony which took place in April 1990.

After the ceremony we approached the newly elected county supervisor about the possibility of giving free outdoor concerts to the public. She went along with the idea and presented it to Jim Ronstadt, director of Tucson Parks and Recreational Department, for his approval. At the time, the city was under heavy criticism for wasting money in the city's northeast wealthy neighborhood, while the poorer neighborhoods in other part of the city were neglected. To give free concerts in the park by the Symphonic Winds came as a blessing and saving grace to the city's officials and the people in charge of the parks. The facilities were to be used for a good cause by offering free performances to the community, thus in May 1990 the "Music in the Park" concert series began and the

Arizona Symphonic Winds

Arizona Symphonic Winds became the official music provider. Our concerts were to be on Saturday nights to avoid conflict with the Tucson Pops Orchestra that performed on Sundays.

We did lots of advertising by placing A-frame posters painted by Mary at the corner of Sabino Canyon and Tanque Verde Roads. After each concert the size of the audience grew and before we knew it the small amphitheater held thousands of people enjoying the music by the Arizona Symphonic Winds. People came with their lawn chairs, blankets, and picnic baskets, both young and old, many with their families.

It is interesting to note that our very first concert at Udall was rained out. As people were driving into the park that rainy evening, Mary and I were standing there with our umbrella telling people, "Sorry, we have no control over the weather, but be here next week." We all smiled, although I was disappointed for not being able to perform, a performance I was truly looking forward to.

Next evening, Sunday, I went to the Tucson Pops concert at Reid Park. The weather was beautiful; not a single cloud to be seen anywhere. The husband of one of the Pops' musicians came over to me and with a sarcastic smile on his face told me that last night's rainout was an "omen," a warning to not mess around with Bucky Steele and his Tucson Pops.

After thirteen seasons with more than 100 free concerts at Udall, the concerts of the Arizona Symphonic Winds remain among the most popular musical events in Tucson during the late spring and early fall. During the last sixteen years the Symphonic Winds has performed more than 250 concerts. It's quite an accomplishment and I'm very proud of it. Mary played an important role and was a large contributor to the success of the organization by being the group's manager. She also did much of the behind the scenes work for many years, until our divorce. Highly dedicated band members carry on the continued success of the Winds and some of them go way beyond the call of duty. People like Sandy Weber, Sherry

Jameson, Al Vreeland, Fred Peryer, Serena Baker, Lois Burke, and Patrick Montoya are just a few of the people who cannot be thanked enough. All musicians in this band are unpaid, volunteering their time and talents to provide beautiful music to the public. I'm truly grateful for their dedication.

Tom Eglin

Arizona Symphonic Winds in Udall Park

Arizona Symphonic Winds, 2001

I would also like to thank the Tucson Parks and Recreation Department for sponsoring the Winds for the Udall Park concerts. For a few years Tucson's newspaper, *The Arizona Daily Star,* provided sponsorship for us by giving free advertising in the paper. Those advertisements helped greatly in attracting big audiences to the concerts. We would be honored to have them sponsor us again.

Since the beginning of the Arizona Symphonic Winds concert series at the park I have been asking for a band shell to be built to improve the sound of the band. I have received only promises so far from the city's officials. A band shell with its acoustics would greatly enhance the sound quality of the band, providing greater enjoyment for the audience. In the meantime, I just keep on dreaming.

Fundraising for KUAT (PBS)-TV, Tucson, 2002

From the time when they were six years old, as a birthday present I let both André and Daniel on their respective birthdays, get in front of the band to conduct a march during the outdoor fall concerts at Udall Park. They do keep a good beat but most of the time they have the tendency to slow down the tempo as their arms get tired. After the march is over they turn to the audience to take a bow. The band members and people in the audience love those boys. Both boys have been attending rehearsals and concerts since the day they were born. During rehearsals, unless sleeping, they used to crawl between musicians, exploring the territory.

At the Udall Park outdoor concerts we would set up a playpen right in front of the staging area for them and that is where they stayed during the performance. We had many volunteers from the audience who were most willing to watch over them. As the boys grew they started to climb out of the playpen and I had to turn around many times throughout the performance to see where they were. Mary, playing clarinet in the group at that time, kept a steady eye on them also.

One night after intermission I was looking for Daniel but couldn't find him. He was about three years old at the time. I told the audience that I would not start the program until Daniel was found. Everybody looked everywhere including the men's restroom. Finally one of the musician's daughters came down the aisle with Daniel walking next to her. There was a great relief. She told me that Daniel had to go to the bathroom and she took him to the ladies' room. I told the audience that my son was discovering girls at an early age, producing a big laugh from them. Even today, many of the concert goers remember the boys fondly in the playpen and recall Daniel's visit to the ladies' room.

There were many instances when my "slip of the tongue" caused much rousing laughter from the audience. Once I was explaining to the audience that before each concert the musicians spend a great deal of time playing before the performance to warm up. Without realizing what I said there was tremendous laughter coming from the band members and from the audience. I turned to the musicians asking, "What the hell did I say this time that is so funny?" They couldn't stop the laughter and many of them were wiping the tears out of their eyes caused by the hilarity. Finally one of them told me what happened. Instead saying "playing before" I said "foreplay." I cracked up laughing myself. It took some time before the concert resumed.

Arizona Symphonic Winds

On another occasion I was explaining the musical form "Rondo." "First there is a melody, we call it section 'A', and when it is finished a new tune comes in, calling it 'B.' Then the section 'A' is repeated and when it's done another melody is introduced and we call it 'C' section." This time I realized what I said and added, "That doesn't sound right, does it?" Again, big laughter from everybody.

During one of the performances there was too much talking noise coming from the audience. I stopped conducting and the band members looked at me, puzzled. I turned to the unruly audience and delivered a sermon, telling them that we worked very hard in preparation for this program; we have a great number of people who would like to enjoy the music we provide, however, some individuals have no concern and respect for the enjoyment of others. "The constant talking exhibited by some of you is very disturbing to the musicians who try to concentrate on their performance," I said. "The following speech was delivered by the famous conductor Leopold Stokovsky to a noisy audience, 'A painter paints his pictures on canvas. But musicians paint their pictures on silence. We provide the music, and you provide the silence.'" My talk was followed by a tremendous ovation from the audience, while the band members looked at me in disbelief. Every three to four years I have to lecture the audience about proper concert behavior. One time I had to yell at André and Daniel for being noisy and said, "You should know better than to mess around." One day at the supermarket a lady came up to me and said, "Maestro, I was one of the talkers during the concert last night and I'm very sorry."

I was conducting the regional honor high school orchestra and after the final run-through before the concert the players had about two hours of free time. I tried to tell them that they should look over and practice their individual parts so we could have a fine performance. However, I ended up saying, "You should look over your private parts." There was a huge outburst of laughter everywhere and years later I'm still reminded about my "slip of the tongue."

The Arizona Symphonic Winds provide an incredible service to our community, but what does it provide the players? Jerry Gary, one of our trumpet players, expressed himself to me in the following e-mail: "Let me assure you that I truly love and respect our ASW. It saw me through some very difficult times in my life...always a steady resource in a sometimes turbulent and unsteady environment. During my days at Hughes Aircraft, when the pressure of preparing, submitting, and negotiating contracts with the Air Force and the Army was so extreme, I never missed a rehearsal or a performance, because those few hours allowed me to free my mind of the stress and details and to immerse myself in something beautiful. So, thank you Maestro."

Thank you, members of this fine musical organization, for letting me be your maestro throughout the years.

"America, the Beautiful"

Our repertoire at Udall Park consists of a variety of different types of music: overtures, rousing marches, selections from Broadway musicals, popular tunes, and waltzes. Soloists include young, talented students as well as professionals. I try to make it enjoyable to the public who take their time to come and hear us.

I am an entertainer and an educator. While I entertain my audience I also try to educate them by playing some of the classics. I explain and direct their attention to what to listen for in the music, and for this they thank me. I want them to learn something they never knew before and they appreciate it greatly.

I also decided that all of our outdoor concerts would start with the "Star Spangled Banner" and end with "America, the Beautiful." This tradition is still going on. During the rendition of "America, the Beautiful," I turn to the audience to encourage them to sing along with the band. Week after week I started to notice

Arizona Symphonic Winds

that during our closer, some people in the back stood in attention. As time went by more and more people were imitating them and before I realized it, the whole audience was standing and singing. Over 100 concerts later all I have to do is to point to the timpani player for the opening roll and the standing up is automatic. After the introduction of the "America, the Beautiful" I turn around to cue the audience to sing with us. As I look at the wall-to-wall people standing, giving homage to this great country, it puts tears in my eyes. All of us at that moment are giving thanks, counting our blessings for being able to live in a free country. The reaction of the audience is the same at the Tucson Pops concerts in Reid Park. Ever since Labor Day weekend in 2001, I close the program with a rendition of "God Bless America."

At first, during the band's performance of the "America, the Beautiful," the audience began folding their lawn chairs and slowly left the amphitheater. For many of them the music became background music or "traveling music." That was not my intention when I decided to close our programs with that patriotic piece of music. The following week I turned to the audience and gave a short talk about what "America, the Beautiful" means to me. Although I do not remember my exact words that night, the basic message was: "America, the Beautiful" has a very special meaning to many. This country represents freedom. This country opened its doors to me, gave me a chance to better myself, and do whatever I wanted in life. I felt fortunate to come here. Remember when I first stepped off from the airplane, I dropped on my knees and kissed the ground of this great country? To me, this musical composition is like a prayer, giving thanks to this country of ours that provides so much opportunity, possibility, and above all, freedom. Where I came from none of the above was available to the people. How lucky and fortunate we all are.

From that night on nobody moved, just sat in silence while the music was being played. I was encouraging the audience to sing along, and slowly the singing became more and more audible.

No Regrets

After the concert many people came up to me, thanking me for the speech and for opening up the eyes of many. One of them said, "It takes a foreigner to tell us Americans about America, this great land of ours, and point out how fortunate we are." A lawyer acquaintance of mine told me the following one day: "When I hear "America, the Beautiful" being played by the Arizona Symphonic Winds with László conducting, I see a young man walking in the back streets in a communist country growing up under depressed conditions. Then I see this same young man grown up years later telling and showing us Americans what a wonderful country we live in and how blessed we are."

Tucson High School and the famed Steel Band

After spending a year at Palo Verde High School, I moved to Rincon/University High for a year. While there, two former teacher colleagues of mine, Larry Williams and Karen Husted, approached me from Tucson High Magnet School. Both used to be on the faculty at Santa Rita when I was there and we were good colleagues. Over breakfast they told me about Tucson High, and with their great sales job they managed to lure me to the school where they were holding positions of Assistant Principal and Director of Fine Arts respectively. I remained at Tucson High for next twelve years, until my retirement from teaching in the public schools.

I took over the music program which was pretty abysmal at the time. The school had not had a regular band director for the last three or four months of the 1986-87 school year. The students were great and the parent organization most helpful in the transition. The band improved with great leaps from one day to the next, and in a short time became competitive. As far as being a concert band, we played as well as any other school in town, and without bragging, better than most. During my tenure the concert band constantly received the rating of "Superior with Distinction" at regional music

Arizona Symphonic Winds

festivals under the auspices of the state.

I was approached many times by Ed Arriaga, principal of the school, posing the question, "What could our magnet school offer to our students that other schools are not capable of in the music department?" One day Mary suggested steel drums. I said, "What the hell are steel drums?"

In 1989, the University of Arizona started a steel band program and I got in touch with an old colleague, Gary Cook. Gary was the head of the percussion department and told me a few things about the instruments. The drums were made out of fifty-five-gallon oil barrels cut to different lengths, and with the use of a hammer concaved at the top to certain depths, followed by precision tuning. Years later I attended a workshop given by Ellie Mannett in West Virginia, where I had the opportunity to observe the building and tuning of the drums. Very fascinating!

After talking to Gary, I went home and a requisition was put together and presented to Ed the next day. The cost of a start-up steel band was $6,000. I told him that the builder of the drums, Ellie Mannett, was the best in the business and required cash up front with a year of waiting for the delivery.

This took place in the fall of 1989. I forgot about the whole thing until I received an urgent call from the administration in early April 1990. I was told that there was grant money available for the purchase of the drums. However, the money had to be used by June 30 or the grant was lost. In panic I picked up the phone and talked to Kaethe George, Ellie's secretary, and business manager. I told her about my dilemma and the urgency behind it. Kaethe promised that she would call me back first thing in the morning.

The call came and I was told that except for one instrument, all others would be available for pickup by the first week of May. I know what happened. Ellie was building drums for somebody else, but because of the pressure from me plus the cash, I was to receive somebody else's order.

Ellie was born in Trinidad, considered to be the "father" of the modern steel drums and supreme authority of the instrument. He had a shop set up in Phoenix, not too far for us to pick up the newly-built instruments. Sure enough, the instruments arrived as promised a few days before the summer break.

I called Gary to send me some players from the university to demonstrate the drums for the students by playing a few tunes. There was tremendous excitement among all of us and we were excitedly looking forward to the beginning of the school year in September. In the fall of 1990 the Tucson High Steel Band program was established and within a few years became one of the most beloved performing groups in the city and the surrounding communities, performing over sixty public performances per year in front of thousands of people. The group became a regular feature at the Udall Park concerts and at Reid Park, performing with the Tucson Pops Orchestra, and receiving huge ovations. Although I retired from teaching four years ago, people still ask me about the Tucson High Steel Band.

I spent the summer of 1990 listening to music from the West Indies, mainly from Jamaica as sung by Harry Belafonte. I took some of the tunes from the LP records and arranged them for the band. All of the songs had the "calypso" rhythm and when school started I was teaching the tunes like "Jamaican Farewell," "Dolly, Dawn," "Day O," "Brown Skinned Girl," to the enthusiastic students.

Before I knew it, I was creating my own compositions for the group and to my surprise some of them turned out to be very good (while some were bad or so-so). At first my biggest problem was to come up with a title for my new works. Two of my earlier compositions were named after my children: "Cancion de André" and "Song for Daniel." Later on I used my students' names for titles, putting two or three names together to create a title for the song. Students were eagerly looking forward to my new compositions, impatiently waiting to find out whose names would be on the title page. Eventually the group produced a CD which sold very well, and the profits were used to purchase additional instruments, a drum set, case covers, and for tuning.

At first I was hesitant to go to Tucson High when the job was offered to me. Tucson High is an inner city school, and at the time it had a reputation that wasn't very favorable. For an outsider the school was known to have gangs and constant fights. At the school I met some of the finest, highly qualified teachers, a credit to their profession. The administration was supportive; students were nice and at least in my music classes, well behaved and willing to learn. With the steel band program it didn't take me long to realize that by taking the group out to the community I could erase the school's negative image. By the time I retired from teaching in 1999, one of the finest music programs in the city had been created, all with the help of my students who participated. In the process both the students and the school gained much respect from the community. I am very proud of that!

In summing up my teaching career the following quote expresses my belief:

> A hundred years from now it will not matter
> what my bank account was,
> the sort of house I lived in,
> or the kind of car I drove…
> but the world may be different
> because I was important in the life of a child.
> Anonymous

Foothills Phil Intergenerational Orchestra

In the fall of 1992 I received a call from the Catalina Foothills Community Schools informing me about the formation of an orchestra that would eventually introduce the string program in the Foothills School District at the elementary and later at the high school level. I was asked if I had any desire to lead this newly formed group. My reply was a definite no, citing my full schedule that was keeping me very busy.

A few days later I received a call from Maestro Robert Bernhardt, at the time conductor of the Tucson Symphony. He did a good sales job about this new orchestra and after talking to him I decided that I should take a keen interest, for in due course André and Daniel would be attending the same school district. To attract musicians, Bob ran the first introductory rehearsal. I wasn't there, but was told that they had only a handful of string players, but had a lot of wind players including twenty-four flutes.

After being interviewed by Joan Marrs, director of the community schools, I took the position, knowing well what I had to face. At the first rehearsal under my direction we had players of different ages and capabilities. The concertmaster was a twelve-year-old youngster leading the violin section of about five players. We had some fairly decent players that carried the fledgling orchestra, one of them being an oboe player. She was a surgeon doing her residency and would come only when she could get away from the hospital. To help out in the upper string section, I asked some of the better flute players to play violin parts. We were on our way! With patience and encouragement on my part, every rehearsal showed a steady improvement. For our debut concert I invited some of the players I had in the Philharmonia to help us out. Some of the pieces we played at that concert were selections from "Phantom of the Opera," "Carmen Suite" by Bizet, and many others.

I called my long-time best friend Frances (six years later to be my wife), a violinist with the Tucson Symphony, and asked if she would be willing to run some of the string sectional rehearsals. I told her that we needed her guidance and know-how. Since she was a high school orchestra teacher with elementary school experience also, she would be the perfect choice if she was available. She agreed to offer her expertise and ten years later still coaches the strings. Two years ago she was named assistant conductor of the orchestra.

Arizona Symphonic Winds

Since the birth of the orchestra over ten years ago, the string section has grown from a handful of string players to about fifty, and at the same time the total number of musicians has increased to ninety-plus players. The age spread of the players is from ten years old all the way up to seventy-nine. This is truly an intergenerational orchestra and I congratulate Joan Marrs, and the Catalina Foothills Community Schools, for having the foresight to create this much-needed, worthwhile musical organization. For the past ten years orchestra manager, Judi Botwin, has kept the orchestra together and made my job easy by doing the behind-the-scenes work. This is one of the finest activities being offered to the community.

Both André and Daniel are members of the orchestra, and my granddaughter Kayleen, a flute player, used to be a member.

Foothills Phil Orchestra

No Regrets

Tucson Pops Orchestra

The Tucson Pops is a professional orchestra that presents free concerts to the public. In 1990, the orchestra was carrying out a search for a conductor who would eventually replace Charles "Bucky" Steele after his retirement as conductor of the orchestra. Pops orchestra members were asked to submit names as possible candidates for the job. There were five or six names suggested and they were asked to do one concert with the orchestra at Reid Park in the span of about two years. My name got on the list.

We were responsible for building our own program, running the rehearsal, and conducting the concert. After that the orchestra members would vote to decide who the next conductor would be. I felt that my presentation went well and felt good about the overall performance.

Tucson Pops audiences average 8,000-plus.

Eventually I received the notification that I was chosen to be Bucky Steele's assistant conductor. My responsibilities were to

Arizona Symphonic Winds

conduct one piece in every concert in the spring series and slowly take over the fall series. In the spring of 1992 I began my association and tenure with the orchestra. In June 1997 Bucky Steele retired as conductor of the Pops, after leading it for twenty-five years. During his tenure he had built a large audience with his pops-type programming. His wife Jeanne was the announcer, and the two of them were well liked by the masses. Together, with the help of Pops' board president Dave Sitton and executive director Dorothy Spence, they offered many enjoyable musical experiences to hundreds of thousands of people and I admire their dedication for this beautiful cause.

Ready to give out programs and schmooze with the crowd before a Tucson Pops Orchestra concert at Reid Park.

No Regrets

Cleaning the pool before leaving to conduct a concert, 2001.

Euphoria from the Tucson Pops' sound

17

John Philip Veres, King of the Tucson Bandstand

The Critics Speak

In the fall of 1997 I took over as full-time music director and conductor of the Tucson Pops Orchestra. In the *Arizona Daily Star*, Tucson's premier newspaper, the following appeared, written by music critic Ken Keuffel Jr. "...On Sunday, László Veres begins his first season as conductor of the Tucson Pops Orchestra. And because he already heads the Arizona Symphonic Winds, some have anointed him King of the Bandstand." I guess the title was bestowed upon me because of all the concerts I do in the park the old-fashioned way.

Daniel Buckley, music critic of the *Tucson Citizen* newspaper wrote in 1999, "...László Veres...no one has had more impact on the musical quality of life of both young and old in Tucson...he has become the John Philip Sousa of Tucson, entertaining families and retirees as he gives amateurs and semi-professional musicians a worthy outlet...As tireless as he is talented, the Hungarian-born clarinetist is a charismatic figure who has brought honor and distinction to his adopted home."

I take satisfaction in knowing that by providing free concerts for the public, both the Tucson Pops and the Arizona Symphonic Winds offer an incredible service to the metropolitan Tucson population. Not too many cities in the nation offer such a service to its community. My hope is that this worthwhile event will be carried on for many generations to come.

Sousa-type uniform for the Veteran's Day concert with the Arizona Symphonic Winds, Nov. 2002

After taking over the Tucson Pops I slowly brought in Tucson Symphony players in key positions, greatly improving the orchestra's level of playing. Considering the limited amount of time that is available to prepare a concert, both groups do a very commendable presentation. As soloists with the ASW and Pops orchestra I feature top-notch professionals from outside and within the orchestra, also young highly talented musicians from the local high schools. Nancy Davis Booth has been a regular with the Pops for the past twenty-plus years, thrilling the audience with her lovely voice; David Syme, pianist par excellence, is a great favorite also. In addition I'm a great advocate of presenting young gifted performers to the public with both ASW and the Pops.

One of my favorite soloists, Michael Hester, a world-class saxophonist, after our special Sousa concert, Nov. 2002

During Memorial Day weekend, my programming has featured many patriotic type compositions, among them Copland's "Lincoln Portrait" a few times with Congressman Jim Kolbe as narrator. He does have a wonderful feel for the text and his delivery of the passages is convincing. Of course, Sousa's stirring march, "The Stars and Stripes Forever," is always performed at these concerts.

By the end of the 2002 season I had conducted over sixty-five free performances with the Tucson Pops Orchestra at Reid Park, and over 100 free concerts at Udall Park with the Arizona Symphonic Winds. In the past thirteen seasons, before well over a quarter of a million appreciative people, I'm truly grateful to the many musicians who have made all those concerts possible.

There have been quite a few times when I was asked to guest conduct the Tucson Symphony Orchestra. (They still ask.) My wife Frances is a violinist of this very fine symphony. Twice I have conducted the orchestra in concert with no rehearsal. The performances went very well both times. Other times I usually conduct Pops-type concerts, a mixture of light classics, popular Broadway medleys, with soloists.

U.S. Congressman Jim Kolbe narrated Copland's "Lincoln Portrait," Spring 2000.

One of my favorite soloists was John Denman, a great artist on the clarinet. He had performed many times with the Tucson Symphony, Tucson Pops, and the Arizona Symphonic Winds with me conducting. As an artist I thought the world of John's mastery of the instrument. He was able to play both musical genres, the classics and jazz, extremely well. On his final appearance in public before his death he performed his newly composed work, "Crossover Concerto," with the Tucson Pops on September 23, 2001, in front of twelve thousand people with me as conductor. The "Crossover" is a combination of the classics and jazz. It was an incredible evening I shall never forget. He was a very sick man—the cancer was eating him away—but his performance that evening was the effort of a superhuman person. He could hardly take breaths and his voice was almost inaudible. I knew during the performance as he was struggling with his health problems that he would never play again. With that performance he was saying good-bye to this world.

Back stage with John Denman, 1995

A few days before his rehearsal with the orchestra, I got together with him and his wife, Paula Fan, at their home to familiarize myself with the concerto. He was sitting on a high padded chair, which was unusual for he always stood when playing the clarinet. Between each movement he had to stop to catch his breath and to clear his throat. It was obvious that he was in terrible pain. After running through the whole piece he did not care to play it again, which was also unusual for John. It is possible that he trusted me; after all, he soloed at least thirty times in the past with me as conductor. At the end of the session I noticed that the concerto was dedicated to Buddy DeFranco, probably the greatest jazz clarinetist of all time. I asked John if Buddy knew about the dedication to which he replied, "He can't wait to get hold of the piece." I told John that Buddy DeFranco was an idol of mine and especially of my brother, Zoltán.

During the rehearsal with the orchestra he did not care to repeat any part of the first movement. That was unheard of in the past. We played the second movement and again he said to go on. I wasn't used to comments like that coming from John. He had always had plenty of things to say and many times he acted like a prima donna in rehearsals. We were into the third movement cruising in a fairly good speed when all of a sudden he stopped playing. It took me some time to stop the orchestra. I looked at him and in a soft whispering voice he said, "László, I'm not dead yet." We started the last section again in a faster tempo but those incredibly fast fingers of the past could not handle some of the difficult passages.

For the past few years in the month of January the Tucson Symphony presented a special Pops concert titled, "Evening of Swing with John Denman." John had a large following and the three-night concert was always a total sellout. As John was dying (he died in the first week of November) he contacted his friend Buddy DeFranco to take his place in the January concert. Buddy was to perform the "Crossover" and many other pieces that were John's favorites. I volunteered to conduct the piece since I was familiar with it, but also because I wanted to meet Buddy DeFranco.

For me it was a dream come true. Frances and I invited

Buddy and his wife Joyce to our house for a reception after one of the concerts. They are beautiful people, and talking to Buddy was a joy. He is very humble; one wouldn't know that one was standing front of one of the greatest artists of all times. We also invited a bunch of clarinet players and not one turned down the invitation. We all had a great time and I was flying high in pleasure and delight.

In the spread of less than four months I had the privilege to conduct the "Crossover Concerto" twice with two giants as soloists.

I knew John for over twenty-five years as a friend and colleague. I miss him.

Buddy DeFranco, like John Denman, is a world-class clarinetist, and a special friend. Feb. 2002

18

Frances Ann Upham

My best friend

After knowing each other and being good friends for almost thirty years, Frances and I were married on July 24, 1999, in Tucson. Many people showed up for the wedding including all of our relatives except my mother, who had just had a mild heart attack, and Fran's mother, who had just had open-heart surgery.

The first time I noticed Fran was in 1972 at the Tucson Convention Center Music Hall. We had just finished rehearsal with the Tucson Symphony and I was on my way out from the stage when I heard the sound of a violin coming from the Green Room, located next to the stage across the hallway. I glanced in the room to find out who was practicing after the long rehearsal. In the corner next to the grand piano a pretty girl with blond hair was warming up when Maestro Millar, conductor of the orchestra, walked in with the orchestra's personnel manager. I realized that she was about to take an audition for a position in the orchestra. She sounded good on the violin; it was obvious that she was a fine player with good schooling behind her. I went home wondering who she was.

A few weeks later she was playing in the orchestra and I

kept looking at her during rehearsals and during breaks, slowly building up the courage to talk to her. I really liked her a lot and used to get the shivers when we were close to each other. Eventually with some friends we would go for a pizza and beer after a concert. I found myself talking to her more and more. We saw each other only at rehearsals or at an occasional pizza place after concerts, always with friends present. My marriage to Linda by that time was falling apart. Michael was around nine years old.

I was in love with Fran without her knowing it, although I sensed there was something mutual about our relationship. I felt good while talking to her and being around her. Just seeing her gave me great pleasure.

One day I told her that I longed to marry her. She told me that she wasn't about to break up my marriage to Linda, especially since Michael was still a young boy. I realized that I had responsibilities to live up to, I had a family with a young child who needed a father, but on the other hand I wasn't happy. Her answer to me was a crushing blow at the time; however, we managed to remain friends throughout the years. She had been recently divorced from an abusive husband and was a single mother with a seven-month-old little girl at the time. After her divorce she moved back to Tucson where she was raised.

A few years later she got married and moved out of the state. Periodically she would return to Tucson to visit her parents and occasionally play in the symphony as a substitute in the violin section. Seeing her at times like that always gave me a warm feeling, a feeling that never diminished as years went by. We kept in touch every two or three years on the phone or when she was in town. She was and still is my very best friend. I truly believe that our friendship was always shared and was mutual.

In the middle of the 1980s she settled in Tucson with her husband and started to play in the symphony on a permanent basis. However, by that time I had retired from the orchestra and wasn't playing my clarinet except for fun. In the middle of the 1990s she

No Regrets

became André and Daniel's piano teacher, and the boys studied with her for about three years. The boys liked her and she liked them. After each lesson she and I would visit, while the boys made a mess on the floor with the different toys she had for them.

Ultimately both of us went through a divorce. A divorce always is a painful experience and speaking for myself, I was pretty much bummed out and depressed at the time. Mary told me numerous times as she was slowly drifting away that I should see a psychiatrist due to the many psychological problems I had acquired because of the war. The insurance company granted me three appointments. I knew I had a good head on my shoulders and that I was fine. However, I was looking for a second opinion and assurance. The psychiatrist was one of the very best in the business and was highly recommended by my physician. After the hour-long visit he told me that there was nothing wrong with me and no more visits were necessary unless I wanted to. He also told me that Mary's accusations of my problems were nonsense, unfounded, and in times like a marriage breakup, it is not unusual for the person in the wrong to use all kinds of negative allegations to justify their own attitudes.

Fran was outside waiting for me in the car. On the way out I was dancing, flying high as a kite, and couldn't wait to tell Fran the good news. She said something to the effect of, "I knew it would be a waste of time; there is nothing wrong with you." Nevertheless, I felt good about the doctor's reassurance. Having Fran as a friend at those times was a blessing. We started seeing each other more and more and I knew that in due time we would be married.

While my marriage dissolution was in progress I moved into an apartment complex where I stayed for six months. I had called Mary's father on the phone telling him about the marriage situation and he suggested that I should move out of the house, which I did. Later on I asked myself in puzzlement, "Why me? Mary should have moved out of the house." Ultimately I was glad it was me who moved out, letting the boys stay in the house where they were born, to make their lives as comfortable as possible during the disturbed times. Arizona is a no-fault state and the courts side with the mothers awarding them custody of the children in most divorce cases.

The only material things I took with me were the bed and the recliner chair. It was an unfurnished apartment and felt very lonely. I started buying basic stuff like a broom, dustpan, dishes, and soap. My son Michael and my older brother Zoli were the only relatives of mine who knew about my separation at the time and both were extremely upset. Zoli called me every single day from Los Angeles wanted to know how I was doing. Michael offered his help right away to help me move the few possessions. Zoli sent me a TV, stereo, food processor, and a telephone answering machine to make my stay at the apartment more pleasant. He encouraged me to meet people and not to spend too much time alone in the apartment. He was talking from experience.

One day I told him that I'd been seeing somebody and I was not lonely. He was glad to hear that, but asked a question in a hurry, "Is she over fifty?" I replied yes, she was, and the only thing he said with a smiling voice was, "Tell her I love her!" Michael was constantly checking on me also, and we spent much time at Daniel's Restaurant where he was executive chef at the time. The two of us put away a few glasses of wine during our talks after his working hours and visited many different bars in the process. Both he and Zoli played a major role in making my loneliness as pleasant as possible. I thanked both of them several times.

Fran was out of the state during that time, visiting relatives in South Dakota and in Colorado. I could hardly wait for her return and went to the airport a good hour ahead of the plane's arrival time to pick her up. The date was July 14 and it was a Tuesday night. We were glad to see each other. Destiny finally brought us together, twenty-eight years later.

During those difficult times I did see the boys every day

No Regrets

after school, and they stayed with me every other weekend as mandated by the courts, thus easing my loneliness tremendously. They slept in sleeping bags on the floor during the weekend stays. The poor innocent boys had no idea what was going on, however they handled the situation extremely well. André made the comment that now they would have two homes to live in and twice as many presents at Christmas and birthdays. I liked that attitude. As always, they gave me great pleasure. I love those boys dearly, more than they will ever know.

I introduced Fran to Michael and his wife, Missy, first, and later to my grandchildren, Kayleen and Karylin. They liked her right away. I took Fran to Los Angeles to meet my relatives. She had met Zoli months earlier. When I had moved into the apartment Zoli called me and wanted to know if I was free on a certain day in March. I told him I was and he said, "Good, I have two extra tickets for you to Gershwin's opera 'Porgy and Bess,' and by that time I hope you will bring with you a lady friend." We flew to Los Angeles and Fran met Zoli and his wife, Erzsi, for the first time. Zoli welcomed her with open arms and put her at ease the way only Zoli can do. He has a special gift for that. Erzsi did the same in her friendly way.

In July of the same year came the difficult time: mother had to be told about the divorce and Frances had to be introduced. When she found out, her typical Jewish mother's concern for me was, "Oh my God, there was nobody to take care of you!" Her voice and facial expression showed sadness not because of the divorce necessarily, but because of the condition of my health. She wanted to know how the boys were, but as soon as she saw them she felt a lot better. I introduced Fran to her. She gave Fran a typical mother's welcome hug, and the only thing she said in her characteristic way was, "Welcome, darling, and make sure that you take good care of him." Since that day Fran has been taking good care of me. She met Pista's and Jancsi's family later that day and they welcomed her also in their friendly way. One day I was on the

phone with Pista telling him that I was going to marry Frances, to which he jokingly replied, "You turkey."
Finally the day came when I proposed to her.

Marriage proposal to Frances

On May 9, 1999, at the opening of the spring concerts with the Tucson Pops, we had an estimated audience of eight to nine thousand people in attendance. As I was introducing one of the show tunes I stopped for a moment and after a short hesitation on my part I said the following: "Tonight I would like to share something with you, so please listen for I will not repeat it. I'm getting married this summer, but there is one problem. The lady I plan to marry doesn't know about it yet, so I'll ask her now. "Frances Ann, would you marry me?" Fran, who plays the violin in the orchestra, was totally caught off-guard, but stood up with a face as red as could be and said, "Why not?" Since the audience could not hear her I relayed the message to them using the microphone, "She said yes!" There was a big applause from the audience and also a shock from many. Nobody had ever proposed at a Pops concert before. I continued by saying that the planned date was July 24 and everybody was invited, but I added in a real hurry, that the wedding would take place in Budapest, Hungary. Huge laughter followed the announcement. The following week in the *Arizona Daily Star* newspaper my marriage proposal was mentioned in the editorial pages:

"People at last Sunday's Tucson Pops concert at Reid Park received a special invitation. After conductor László Veres proposed to one of the orchestra's violin players, and she accepted, he invited the entire audience to their summer wedding. The invite was sincere but comes with one hitch: The wedding will be in Veres' home town of Budapest."

For a while this was the talk of the town.
The marriage did take place on the appointed date but

instead of Budapest, it took place in Tucson. All of my brothers were present and all of our children. Michael, André, and Daniel were all dressed in white tuxedo jackets, black trousers, and black bow ties. They looked handsome and they knew it. The next day André suggested that Fran and I should get a divorce. When I asked him why, his answer was very innocent: "So we can have another great party like this."

Fran and I did go to Budapest in the spring of 2001 and had

With my beloved Frances on our wedding day, July 24, 1999

a great time. She fell in love with the city and wants to go back for another visit. I took her to many places including the neighborhood streets where we Veres boys were raised. She truly enjoyed the many beautiful places of interest, buildings, historical sites, and the bridges that span the Danube River joining the two cities, Buda and Pest, into one.

Fran is my perfect partner, a beautiful, loving person with

With my boys and Frances' daughter, Angela Moeckly— left to right: Daniel, André, Michael, July 24, 1999

a great sense of humor. We share our love for each other and she is still my one and only best friend. She loves her extended family, loves André and Daniel, and thinks the world of Michael, Missy, Kayleen, and Karylin. I also love my extended family, "the package," as she calls it. Her daughter, Angela, and her mother, Fern, are lovely people. Angela is an attractive, friendly, smart, charming person with a great sense of humor. Fran takes great pride in her, loves her deeply, and cares about her well-being like most mothers. I as her stepfather, feel closer and closer to her as time marches on.

It took Fran and me almost three decades before we finally married one another, and the result was well worth waiting for. I think we make a perfect pair, if there is such a thing. Thanks to her, I keep the line of communication open with my ex-wives to keep the children happy; after all, they love both of their parents.

The Veres brothers in 1999—left to right: Stephen, John, László, Zoltán, George

My previous wives were wonderful ladies; the problem was that we could not see eye to eye on many of the issues. I liked things my way and they liked things their way. I try to think that I am a flexible person, but I guess neither Linda nor Mary thought so. Frances and I communicate pretty much on the same wavelength. Of course today I'm a lot older and hopefully wiser and mellower than I was forty years ago. Even though two of my previous marriages failed and ended up in divorce, I have no regrets. Both were excellent people; I learned a great deal from them; they were great supporters of me in many of my endeavors and were proud of my achievements. I truly believe that at one point in their life they dearly loved me and they still think fondly of me. There is no question that I loved both of them. I do hope that I had something useful to offer them during our relationship. We have plenty in common: the children will tie us together forever.

Fran has told me many times, "I'm sure glad your ex-wives dumped you. I don't think they realized how lucky they were to have a caring, responsible person like you as a husband. They will have a very difficult time in finding somebody like you again." Each time she mentions that I tell her that I'm a lot older, hopefully wiser, and have changed a lot throughout the years. Her reply is, "People don't change that much, the basic personality traits will always be there." I think she is quite prejudiced and very much partial in her opinions towards me.

The hugging has never stopped. 1999.

Fran wanted to be part of the Arizona Symphonic Winds and wanted to play a wind instrument. Playing violin in the Tucson Symphony wasn't enough for her. I told her that since she could read music she could play the bass drum for we were short of percussion players. She liked the idea but soon found out that

No Regrets

playing the instrument the correct way wasn't easy. She has become a dedicated member of the organization and is willing to carry the heavy instrument to concerts. Of course an SUV had to be purchased to haul the instrument. Presently Fran is the president of the Symphonic Winds and does a fine job in her position.

Her full-time job is teaching in the public schools. For the past nineteen years she has been the orchestra director at Rincon/University High School and during her tenure she has created one of the finest string programs in the state of Arizona. She is a dedicated teacher and a credit to her profession. There is a great need for more highly qualified teachers like her.

Frances donned a sari for the wedding of my niece, Amy, in Edmonton, Alberta.

19

Béla and Klára Veres

My parents

I have a few heroes I admire: Abraham Lincoln, John F. Kennedy, Beethoven, and some other people who greatly contributed to the human spirit. But, if I would have to pick two heroes, without hesitation it would be my parents. During my sixty-five years I have never met gutsier, braver, stronger-willed, harder working, more loving and courageous people than them. To them the survival of the family came first and all the sacrifices they made were for the children. They had more common sense than most people I have known.

My father was a strong disciplinarian and had a mind of his own. I don't necessarily agree with his philosophy that preaches the idea that only men are rulers of the house; everything had to be done his way without questioning the decision with total obedience or else (remember the movie "Fiddler on the Roof"?). I have to remember the times he lived in and also where he was living. Hungary and the old customs are not the way of life in the United States and the two cannot be compared. While my mother did adapt to the American way of life fairly quickly, my father had a difficult time adjusting to it, especially with the question on how we children should be raised.

With my parents in 1971

We children, all grown, will never understand our parents' hard times and difficult conditions throughout WWII, which includes Hitler and the Nazis; and after the war Stalin and the communists, and the toll all that took on them, particularly on our father. We'll never understand the hardships on him while he was a soldier in the Hungarian Army. How he had to report many times for military duty, leaving a wife with young children behind, not knowing if he would ever return. How he fought on the Russian front and was part of the Hungarian army when they were retreating after the Soviet Army defeated the Germans. As the Russian Red Army was forcing the German and Hungarian Army to retreat (Hungary joined the Germans in the fight against Russia, thinking that they would beat them, but they were proven wrong), many of my father's soldier comrades froze to death on the frozen fields in the process. Many perished from having no food, shelter, or will-power for survival. Surely these situations affected him; disturbed the progress of his and his wife's lives. On the other hand, at the same time it made both of our parents stronger people and survivors! Will we children ever understand and comprehend all this?

My mother, still classy at age 90, June 2002

I feel honored and privileged to have Béla and Klára Veres as my parents. I cherish the countless valuable lessons they taught me. I used their ideas, adopted many of them and discarded some of them. I became a better teacher in the classroom because of them. I was strict with my students and never had disciplinary problems with them. I demanded excellence from the students,

No Regrets

but I also loved them. I received the greatest respect from them and in many cases was idolized by them. Even today, I receive letters from former students thanking me for insisting and demanding hard work, discipline and respect. To quote from a letter recently received from a former student: "...I have always wanted to thank you. I want to thank you for your music...for all the fun...for your professionalism...for your demand...the passion you had for music...the quality of music you were able to squeeze from a bunch of 'worthless teenagers'...forging respectable citizens out of us..." (Most of these students are now in their forties with families of their own). Deep down I know that my parents' influence on me in this respect was very powerful.

This is how I feel about my parents. All my brothers have their own feelings, and their opinions could be a lot different from mine. But I always think of my father and mother with warm thoughts, utmost love, tremendous respect and reverence, and with the greatest of admiration!

The life-saving poem

Here is the poem ("Nemzeti dal") with English translation, that possibly saved our lives from the Nazis when my then nine-year-old brother Zoltán recited it front of them. The young twenty-five-year-old patriotic poet Sándor Petőfi wrote the "National Song" and delivered it on March 15, 1848, during the eve of the Hungarian uprising against the Austrian Hapsburg Empire in front of thousands of people. He died in battle the following year. The poem can be compared to the French "La Marseillaise."

Nemzeti dal
Petőfi Sándor verse

Talpra Magyar, Hí a haza!
Itt az idö, most vagy soha.

Béla and Klára Veres

Rabok leszünk vagy szabadok?
Ez a kérdés, válaszatok!
A Magyarok istenére Esküszünk,
Esküszünk, hogy rabok továb Nem leszünk!

National Song
Poem by Sándor Petöfi

Rise up, Magyar, the country calls!
It's "now or never" what fate befalls...
Shall we live as slaves or free men?
That's the question - choose your "Amen!"
God of Hungarians,
we swear unto Thee,
We swear unto Thee - that slaves we shall
no longer be!

Epilogue

I am now sixty-five years old, and as I look back and relive my past, I can honestly say that I have no regrets. I did everything the very best way I could. I made some mistakes along the way. However, that is part of the learning process.

Even in the most difficult times I enjoyed my childhood. I did not enjoy washing the kitchen floor every day as a ten or twelve year old, but it had to be done. With all the chores we had to do, we still had plenty of time to be children and have fun. We were very creative in coming up with different types of games. We children didn't know that there was a better life someplace else in the world. It was the adults that did all the suffering during World War II, the Nazi and the communist régimes. I don't ever recall being hungry; somehow there was always food available for us provided by our parents. We always had clothing and even though my parents didn't have much money, when we left the apartment my mother made certain we looked clean and well groomed.

I enjoyed my teenage years. I enjoyed being both an automobile mechanic and a soccer player, and enjoyed learning a musical instrument. I enjoyed the many movies, operettas, operas, and all the international soccer games or track and field com-

Epilogue

petitions I was able to attend. We had a beautiful radio and record player and I took great delight listening to music. I remember well one night being home with my younger brothers who were asleep. I was glued to the radio with the volume turned low, listening to beautiful operatic music. I was totally immersed and didn't even hear my parents walk in. The performance had just ended and it was Puccini's opera, "La Boheme." From the beauty of the music I must have had tears in my eyes because my mother wanted to know what was wrong. Those years truly went by fast.

My escape from Hungary in 1956 was no big deal. I looked at it as a great adventure. I was young and was eager to visit the places I had heard so much about. My six-month stay in Vienna was fun, and my early years in the United States, with all the difficulties, were just a new chapter in my life. I learned to adapt very fast, and learned the language to get ahead in life. I enjoyed the military including basic training with all the harassment that goes with it. Thank God, I was blessed with a positive attitude.

I loved my years as clarinetist in the symphony and I truly loved being a teacher. I was called a "born teacher" by one of my professors during my student years. Was I a born teacher? I don't know; on the other hand, I do know that I had the knack to excite young people for learning and bring out the best from them.

I learned a great deal from my students throughout my teaching years. During my "green years" as a teacher one of my student told me, "Mr. Veres, don't try to be our friends, we have our own friends." I found out in a hurry that using sarcastic words causes more harm than good and that one can't judge a book by it's cover. During one of the early years I got angry at the band during rehearsal and walked out on the students. As I look back I truly made a first-class fool out of myself. At the end of the school year a graduating senior boy told me, "Mr. Veres, I have all the respect for you as a teacher and musician, but when you walked out on us, my great respect for you diminished." That comment coming from one of my students was a very humbling experience

No Regrets

for me. I also discovered along the way that students appreciated discipline, order, professionalism, and the expectation for excellence that was demanded from them. I also found out that a smile, positive attitude, enthusiasm, and love of the subject matter is contagious. They craved to be guided, cared for, loved, respected, and in return they would do anything for you including playing their hearts out during a performance. My students made me a better teacher; without me realizing it, they were shaping and molding me throughout my teaching years. I learned a great deal from them and I learned from my own mistakes.

I enjoy being a conductor and take great pleasure bringing beautiful music to audiences. I love music with a passion, and when I'm conducting I put all my heart and soul into the performance. I hope I never loose that enthusiasm, and I also hope that I will always remain a teacher. When I'm on the podium conducting concerts, I love teaching the audience about music. I guess I'll always remain an educator.

I feel honored that I been asked numerous times to guest conduct the Tucson Symphony Orchestra, the Southern Arizona Symphony Orchestra, the Flagstaff High School Summer Camp Bands, the Rocky Ridge Music Center Orchestra in Colorado, the TUSD Meritorious Orchestra, Arizona Regional High School Honor Bands and Orchestras, and to be asked many times to be an adjudicator at music festivals. I have received many accolades during my teaching career, including the Arizona Excellence in Music Education Award, Distinguished Alumni and Nunamaker Director's Award of Distinction from the University of Arizona, Southeastern Arizona High School Band Director of the Year Award, and the Outstanding Community Service Award from the Arizona Parks and Recreational Department.

I have no regrets about my failed marriages; my ex-wives are fine ladies and good people. Both of those marriages produced my three beautiful boys whom I passionately love.

I have retired from public school teaching but I'm busier

Epilogue

then ever. I love my life the way it is, and I love my wife Frances. Having her as a partner is like a dream come true.

Having Michael, André, and Daniel as my children is more than anything I could have ever asked for; my boys and my wife are the joys of my life.

I feel blessed!

"Good night, and God bless America."